WORK
Like Your Dog

 *Villard   New York*

WORK
Like Your Dog

Fifty Ways to Work Less,

Play More, and Earn More

Matt Weinstein and Luke Barber

VILLARD BOOKS and colophon are registered trademarks
of Random House, Inc.

Library of Congress Cataloging-in-Publication Data
Weinstein, Matt.
Work like your dog: fifty ways to work less, play more, and earn more /
Matt Weinstein and Luke Barber.
p.   cm.
ISBN 0-812-99199-0
1. Quality of work life.   2. Work environment.   3. Leisure.
4. Hours of labor.   5. Job satisfaction.   6. Industrial management.
I. Barber, Luke.   II. Title.
HD6955.W45   1999
650.1—dc21   98-45463

Random House website address: www.atrandom.com
Printed in the United States of America on acid-free paper
23456789

Book design by Mercedes Everett

To Ritch Davidson, Fran Solomon, and Terry Sand, who
make every day Fun at Work Day for me.
M.W.

To Lee, for her sustaining love and certain wisdom, for
her understanding of the way I walk the earth, and—
most of all—for her gentle acceptance of life with a fool.
To Kurt Vonnegut, simply because he was the first person
ever to dedicate a book to me.
L.B.

Contents

I. *The Game of Work*

II. *Turn Problems into Opportunities*

III. *Learning to Laugh and Play with Life*

I

The
Game of Work

1

Treat
Work as a Game

Many years ago I had a strange dream in which the ancient philosopher Plato called me on the telephone. Collect. This guy calls me all the way from Athens, Greece, in 375 B.C., and he has the nerve to reverse the charges.

Big spender that I am, I accept the call.

In the dream, Plato tells me that he has been asked to make a speech at Aristotle's birthday party and he doesn't have any ideas. He wants to know if I can help him out. So I give him the line "What, then, is the right way of living? Life must be lived as play." He was very excited by the idea and promised to call me back and let me know how it all worked out, but he never did.

Several years later I was thumbing through Plato's *Dialogues* and was astonished to discover that precise quote. I told some of my colleagues about it, and they insisted that I must have subconsciously known about Plato's statement before my dream, even though I had no conscious memory of it.

I myself think the guy ripped me off.

Now, I'm not altogether sure what Plato meant when he used those lines, but I know what I meant. I meant that the best way to live a joyful, healthy, low-stress life is to choose to see work as a game and ourselves as the players. And whatever happens on the job is just a part of that game.

What are the characteristics of a successful game? First, it should be fun for the players and enriching to their lives, or what's the point of playing? Second, it should have a set of rules and strategies governing it, which we can study in order to play more successfully. This book is intended to be a guidebook for playing the Game of Work.

Let's use tennis as an example. If you are playing a game of tennis and your opponent smashes an ace by you, you have a choice. Clearly there is nothing you can do about the fact that you have been aced—that, as they say, is history. The choice you have is how you respond to the situation.

If you are really playing tennis as a game, then you move over to the other side of the court and wait for the next serve. It doesn't help you or the game to stare at the ground and complain. It doesn't help to smash the turf with your racquet and start making excuses for yourself. As a game player, you need only move to the other side of the court, and—because this is the way the game is set up—you get another chance.

This, I know, seems incredibly simple and obvious. Yet, when our life at work serves us an ace, many of us act as if it's the end of the world. Even the smallest of problems or mistakes can get blown completely out of proportion. We spend all kinds of time and energy living in the past, analyzing, criticizing, making excuses, worrying, and generally making ourselves miserable. What we really need to do is to move to the other side of the court. The game of work lets us try it again. We have the power to choose how we respond to the aces life serves us.

If you treat your work as a game, then as soon as you've been served an ace you can begin to look at the possible responses available to you. You can start by saying, "Well, I certainly loused up that easy sale!" or "That was definitely the worst deal I ever made!" or "Now I can kiss that promotion good-bye!" But if you want your work life to be a joyful game, then you have to start moving forward from there. You have to remember that your goal is to get to the other side of the court and to get on with the game of work.

You can ask yourself, "What can I learn from this so I won't make the same mistake next time?" You can remind yourself that you want to be a person who is constantly growing and improving yourself, and you can't do that if you never take any risks and never make any mistakes. Instead of whining, complaining, or beating yourself over the head with your racquet for messing up, you can say to yourself, "Hey, nobody's perfect— how can I learn from my mistakes if I never make any?"

Turn
Work into Play

From time immemorial, frustrated parents have said the same thing to their children: "Let's play a game called Clean Up Your Room!" Although this popular attempt at parental manipulation seldom works, it does express a wonderful idea—that hard work can be fun and that anything can be turned into a game.

Dr. Ernie Lavorini is a master at bringing play to his work. The first thing I noticed when I walked into Dr. Lavorini's dental office was a large sign on the reception desk that said, BE KIND TO MY EMPLOYEES. I LOVE THEM ALL. ERNIE

The employees in Dr. Lavorini's office have gone river rafting together and have made company outings to places like the racetrack, the water slides, and the Renaissance Pleasure Faire. Every year they all go holiday shopping together and then out to dinner—funded by the office.

"It's so much fun to go into the city at Christmastime," says Ernie. "We never tire of it. We all love the way San Francisco looks lit up at night."

One time Dr. Lavorini even arranged for his employees to be "kidnapped." A bunch of his friends arrived at the office with pillowcases over their heads, herded all the employees into their getaway cars, and spirited them away for a day at the beach.

"But what about all your patients?" I asked Ernie dubiously.

"Oh, the receptionists were in on it." He laughed. "It looked like we had a full day booked, but actually there were no patients scheduled."

Most people don't associate the idea of fun with a trip to the dentist. But Dr. Lavorini tries to make even that unlikely venue an upbeat experience for his patients. One day when I needed to have some emergency dental work, Dr. Lavorini said to me, "You need a crown on one of your teeth. But I'm going to show you how to turn a *have-to-have* situation into a *get-to-have* situation." Ernie explained that he could put a tattoo on the crown, a picture of anything I wanted. And since the crown would be on one of my back teeth, completely out of sight, no one would know about it except for me. And it would be a completely painless tattoo, since he would make it directly on the crown, before it was fitted on my tooth.

I chose a comet—a silver star with a blue and yellow tail streaming out behind it. And I smile every time I look at it—in fact, every time I even *think* about it. It's not that easy to look at, actually—I have to pull my lower lip down with one finger, squeeze up close to the mirror, and squint out of one eye. But it always looks great. And if *tooth, comet, astronomy,* or *tattoo* ever come up in conversation, I can always count on an amazed reaction from anyone I dare to show it to.

Let's put this into perspective: if Dr. Ernie Lavorini could turn something like dental surgery from a *have-to-have* situation into a *get-to-have* situation, then how hard can it be to do the same thing with some difficult situations in your own job? How can you turn some task that you dread into something that you *get* to do? The trick is to bring the elements of a game into your work—to learn to play with your job.

In every office, for example, there are some jobs that no one wants to do but that must be done if the office is to function smoothly. One day Cathy Fleming, the vice president of operations for the Sacramento, California, firm Women Incorporated, thought to herself, "Since somebody has to do it anyway, why not make a game out of it?" So she wrote out eight such tasks on slips of paper, tasks like taking money to the bank, taking mail to the post office, cleaning up the office kitchen, changing the toner in the printer, and refilling the fax machine and the copier with paper. Then she placed each of the slips of paper inside a balloon and inflated all the balloons. One by one each of her coworkers got to pop a balloon and—voilà!—discovered her task for the day.

3

See Every Situation as an Opportunity to Play

One of the main reasons people have difficulty transforming their work into play is that they have bought in to an idea that is as fundamental in the United States as the separation of church and state: that is, the separation of work and play. While there may be good, sound reasons for the separation of church and state, the separation of work and play serves no useful purpose. Unless, of course, one is fond of boredom, misery, and low productivity.

Just as some really unskillful people manage to turn play into work, the really skillful person can turn work into play. One of the first steps comes with a change in attitude; you must see every situation, including situations at work, as an opportunity to enjoy your way to success.

People often say that seeing is believing, but the opposite is also true. What we believe affects what we see. If we are looking for something, we greatly enhance the likelihood of seeing it. This is especially true when we are evaluating whether a situation is potentially enjoyable or boring. If we expect a situation to be good, then we increase the chances that it will be.

The obvious conclusion for those of us who want our work life—and the rest of our life—to be lived joyfully and playfully is that we must be ready to see every situation as an opportunity to play. There may be a few exceptions, of course: I don't go to a funeral expecting it to be a party. Most everyday situations, however, hold the potential for play.

A few years ago, I received a phone call that was obviously a wrong number. I had plenty of time off from work that summer, so I was doing a lot of gardening, and I had just come in from digging in my yard when I received the errant call. A woman's voice asked, "Is this the man who does yards?"

I knew that she must have the wrong number, but since I was actually at that very moment fresh from the experience of doing my own yard (and, I might add, already practicing the principle *See every situation as an opportunity to play*), I responded, "Sure, this is the guy who does yards." She explained that she had gotten my number from a friend, and she wondered if I would be willing to mow and edge her yard.

I told her I could easily work her into my schedule. When she asked my fee, I asked her how much I had charged her friend. Thirty-five dollars, she said, and her yard was about the same size. So I told her that I'd do her yard for thirty-five dollars too. She gave me her address, which turned out to be just a few blocks from my house, in a rather nice, old section of town.

I loaded my mower and other equipment into the station wagon and drove to her house, all the while smiling with considerable joy. She turned out to be a very nice, attractive young woman. As she showed me around her yard, I learned that she was a flight attendant and her husband was a pilot for American

Airlines. They had lost contact with their yardman from the previous summer, and she was quite happy to have discovered me. After I finished her yard she gave it a quick inspection, paid me, and asked if I would be willing to keep her as a customer for the summer. Well, I had gone this far with my play, so I figured, "Why not?" Not only did I do her yard for the entire summer, but she also had several additional little jobs for me every so often—weeding the garden, chopping up dead hedges, things like that.

Near the end of the summer, I was invited to a party at my next-door neighbor's house. My neighbor was the president of a local bank, and this somewhat formal affair was a fund-raising event for one of his associates, who was running for a seat on the city council. I looked around at the assembled guests, and who should I see standing across the room but my one and only customer! I made my way over for a brief chat. We exchanged pleasantries, but no mention was made of the fact that I was her yardman.

Later, my next-door neighbor reported a most perplexing conversation with my customer that went something like this:

She: "Bob, could you tell me what *he's* doing here?"

Bob: "What do you mean? What's wrong?"

She: "I'm just surprised to see my yardman at this kind of party!"

Bob: "Your yardman?"

She: "Yes. He's a yardman, and he does my yard."

Bob: "I think you must be confused. He's a professor. He's not your yardman."

She: "That man right there is my yardman! He's not a professor! He's my yardman!"

Bob: "I assure you that he is a college professor. He's my next-door neighbor."

She: "That's *his* house next door? I can't believe a yardman can afford such a nice house!"

Bob: "I don't know what's going on, but I do know he's
not a yardman."

The next time I showed up to do the yard, my customer was
out the door before I could start the engine on my mower. "Excuse me," she said, "but I'm very confused. Bob told me that
you are a college professor?"

"Yes," I replied innocently.

"Well . . . well . . . I'm just surprised that you would have a
second job as a yardman."

It was time to come clean. I told her that I was not a yardman, but that when she called, she hadn't asked me if I was a
yardman. I explained that she had asked if I was the man who
did yards, and that, in fact, I did yards—mine before she called,
and now mine and hers.

She laughed until she was bent over double. Then I started
laughing too. We both agreed it was pretty funny, and then I
finished her yard. She gave me thirty-five dollars, and I went
home.

I know that neither of us will forget the summer I was her
yardman. Of course, mowing someone else's lawn all summer
long is probably not at the top of your list of what you'd like to
do on your summer vacation. But from all the pleasure I got
that summer from answering a wrong number, it became quite
clear to me that the most unlikely situations can be opportunities to play—even when that play involves lots of hard work.

A corporate culture that supports laughter, play, and celebration doesn't just arise spontaneously in most workplaces.
Most of the time you have to put in a lot of work behind the
scenes to create a fun-filled atmosphere on the job. And just
because something is going to be fun doesn't mean it is going to

be easy. Creating fun at work often involves concentrated effort.

Think about a professional basketball player. Here is someone who in one night's work probably sweats more than many of us do in a whole month. And yet there is general agreement that his version of physical labor is "fun" and "a game." Why can we see his job as a game and not our own? Why should playing basketball be fun and mowing a lawn be work?

No situation or occupation is, in and of itself, inherently playful or fun. I've seen lots of people having a miserable time at the beach, at a birthday party—even at their own wedding. And we've all seen professional basketball players who throw temper tantrums when they miss a shot or get called for a foul.

The fun factor in any given situation comes from inside of us. All it takes is a willingness to see life as a game, and then to play along wholeheartedly, whatever it takes.

Let the games begin!

4

Take Every Opportunity to Celebrate

I am a great believer in celebrating even the tiniest of your successes on the job. Anytime is the right time to celebrate, and any excuse will do. Something as simple as opening a bottle of sparkling apple juice (or champagne, if your corporate culture permits it) every other Friday can be a good first step in creating a celebratory culture in your organization. When you pop the cork and ask your coworkers to join you in toasting the successes and fabulous failures of the past two weeks, you send a clear message that you care about the people with whom you work.

It is important, too, to take the time to celebrate in a creative way the landmark events and service anniversaries in your coworkers' careers. The Western sales staff of Sprint found a unique way to honor the longtime employees in their Hawaii office. According to Eric Tom, vice president of sales, the employees established a Wall of

Fame in the office, and five-year employees got to have a blue handprint, framed and signed, up on the wall. After ten years with the office, the employees, with great fanfare, got to contribute a red handprint.

Michael Osterman, CEO of Boise Marketing Services, believes in celebrating the anniversary of the day that each of his employees was hired. I once accompanied Michael as he made his rounds, congratulating each employee whose anniversary fell during that week. There were one-year anniversaries, two-year anniversaries, and five-year anniversaries, and for each of them Michael arrived at the employee's workstation carrying a Mylar balloon bouquet from which hung assorted candy bars. As he presented each bouquet, he thanked the employee for his contribution to the company and took the opportunity to ask him for feedback on the organization's progress. I was impressed by the ritual and by the opportunity it gave Michael to have one-on-one contact with his employees. As the company grew larger, honoring all the service anniversaries had obviously become a more time-consuming procedure, and I asked Michael if it was still worth it, and if the balloon-bouquet ritual had any downside for him.

His face immediately lit up at the question. "Only one big downside." He laughed. "One time I was held up out of town by bad weather, and my secretary had already gotten a bunch of balloon bouquets together for me for that day. So she stored them in my office overnight, which was the only thing she could do. Unfortunately, she left the door to my office open, and during the night the balloons somehow floated their way out of my office and onto the warehouse floor, and they set off all the motion-detector alarms in the entire building. Our security force arrived armed to the teeth, ready to arrest a band of intruders, and all they could find were a bunch of balloons terrorizing the warehouse!"

Many companies take their most successful salespeople off to island vacations as incentive awards for surpassing their sales quotas. The rationale for this special treatment is that these salespeople directly impact the organization's bottom line. But these rewards for the sales staff can leave other employees—whose contributions are harder to track in terms of profits but no less valuable to the organization—feeling resentful of the special treatment accorded the sales staff. A wonderful thing about celebrating service anniversaries is that everyone in the organization has a chance to receive an award: all you have to do is stick around long enough.

However, just because everyone can eventually achieve this long-term service recognition does not, as I found out in my own company, eliminate feelings of resentment and being "left out" among employees who have not yet reached that goal. In the Playfair organization my official title is emperor. Consequently, employees who reach ten years with the company are inducted into the honorary society known as the Emperor's Court. Each induction is highlighted by a ceremony that is personalized to the honoree, and in which the entire company participates.

One of the things that we are proudest of at Playfair is our retention rate. In part because the organization is so much fun to belong to, with an extremely strong sense of being a member of a team, a very high percentage of people hired into the company stay for ten years and longer. At the most recent of our all-company retreats, seven new members were to be inducted into the Emperor's Court. This would have brought the membership of the Emperor's Court to seventeen, out of a total company of twenty-seven employees.

That left only ten employees in the company with less than a decade of service. When these ten realized that they were soon to be in the minority, they jokingly formed their own secret society, which they called the Peasants' Revolt. The peasants privately asked me to arrive late to the Emperor's Court ceremony, and just before the start of the ceremony, they seized control of the meeting. They claimed to have captured the emperor and to be holding him hostage, and to prove it they passed around computer-generated photographs of me behind bars. They then launched into their "revolting" peasants' dance and theme song, to the astonishment and delight of the assembled emperor's courtiers. Finally, the peasants presented a list of demands, all of which made fun of the existing norms of the group. It is a point of company pride that Playfair serves a health-conscious cuisine at all our company meetings; and so the peasants demanded instead that "from now on there will be lots of red meat at all meals." At which point several of the most senior Emperor's Court members leaped to their feet to announce approvingly, "We're joining with them!"

At the culmination of their uprising, the peasants played an audiocassette, purporting to be a message from the emperor disbanding the Emperor's Court. The message turned out, however, to be a message from Marlon Smith, a member of the company who was working in South Africa at the time and who was therefore unable to attend the retreat in person. Marlon gave an impassioned plea for harmony between the two groups, using as his theme Rodney King's famous phrase, "Can't we all just get along?"

The rest of the peasants, pretending to be completely surprised and visibly moved by Marlon's plea, released the emperor from his imprisonment and then joyfully joined in the remainder of the ceremony, vowing to someday become emperor's courtiers themselves.

By treating the whole matter playfully, the members of the Peasants' Revolt set a wonderful tone of laughter and lightness for the Emperor's Court celebration that followed. But more important, they creatively diffused any tension that existed in the company from setting up a "haves" and a "have-nots" situation. However well-intentioned the creation of the Emperor's Court may have been, on one level the more junior members of the organization felt left out of the club. But the members of the Peasants' Revolt were able to even that score. By their act of revolution they took group focus on themselves and let themselves be "seen" in a position of power by the more senior members of the company, and that, of course, is what recognition is all about.

"It was like being the youngest sibling in a family, and all of a sudden being given a big, loud voice," said Playfair trainer Terry Sand, one of the masterminds behind the revolt. "In a playful way, we got to say to the rest of the company, 'Don't forget about us!' "

By pointing out the negative repercussions of the company recognition policy in a playful way, the members of the Peasants' Revolt were able to bring these feelings to the surface in a nonthreatening manner, rather than letting them fester beneath the surface. And this playful act then allowed them to fully support the initiation ceremony of the new emperor's courtiers. In the end, their mock revolt served to strengthen the sense of team spirit among the company as a whole.

In addition to service anniversaries, many other company celebrations can be enlivened by a sense of playfulness. After the completion of a particularly demanding project, for example, it is important to celebrate the successful accomplishment of the team goal. This celebration can have even more impact when it includes a creative gesture of appreciation from upper management to the team for all their hard work. Such a celebration gives the participants a chance to catch their breath, get reenergized, and move forward with a sense of pride and inspiration.

During the spin-off of Lucent Technologies from AT&T, the 2,100 members of AT&T's controller division clocked over 100,000 hours of overtime, working nights, weekends, holidays, and even days when the offices were officially closed due to bad weather. When New Jersey declared a state of emergency because of severe snowstorms, the controller division associates carpooled with four-wheel-drive vehicles and took up residence in local hotels; some even camped out with sleeping bags in their offices, in order to complete the massive reorganization on time.

The whole organization celebrated the completion of the job with a "Week of 100,000 Thanks." To symbolically kick off the festivities, the division's upper management walked around the offices giving away Nestlé's $100,000 bars to everyone in sight. The comptroller announced mandatory nine-to-five hours for the week (forcing those employees who had worked at least twelve-hour days for months to come in "late" and leave "early" all week). Every day there were different activities scheduled, including picnics, softball games, bowling parties, raffles, ice cream breaks, and a jeans-and-sneakers day. "The whole week served as a nice breather, allowed the tension of the previous months to be alleviated, and enabled people who had worked so hard together to celebrate by having some fun together," commented AT&T's Julie Gardner.

Of course you don't need a reason to celebrate at work—some of the best celebrations can happen for no reason at all, just for the sake of celebrating. Sure, it's fine to celebrate people's birthdays, but what about an *un*birthday party for the entire office? The Xerox-account unit of EDS took that idea from Disney's version of *Alice in Wonderland,* and lunch became a giant tea party, at which employees were asked to wear their wildest hats for a Mad Hatter contest. And sure, the office Christmas party can be fun, but what about the rest of the year? The staff of *Successful Meetings* magazine held a Christmas-in-July party at their offices. Employees dug out their Christmas decorations from storage and strung them around the office, complete with foamy snow in hallways and Christmas-in-July presents under the plastic Christmas tree in the lobby.

A classic moment in the history of celebrating for no reason at all was invented by the employees of A Business Conference Call in Chaska, Minnesota, when they celebrated Bad Hair Day. Manager Betty Kay recounts, "The employees all came to work with their hair covered in scarves, hats, and wild wigs. . . . It was impossible to look around the office without smiling! We all talked about it for weeks afterward—what a fun day it was for us!"

Another truly original celebration was initiated by Women Incorporated, a national membership organization that helps women business owners. The Sacramento, California–based headquarters staff held a "Come Dressed as Your Favorite Holiday" event. Cathy Fleming, the vice president of operations, remembers that one staff member came dressed as the Easter bunny and roamed the halls that day delivering Easter eggs. Another staffer came dressed as a turkey, and another, dressed as Cupid, sent valentines to all her coworkers, with messages like "I love working with you, Michelle, because you are so easy to get along with."

Yet another staffer came dressed in an apron for Mother's Day; one woman with pencils sticking out of her hair represented Secretary's Day; and the woman dressed to honor birthdays (no, she did not come to work in her birthday suit) invited everyone to play pin the tail on the donkey in her office. When the final staff member arrived at work that day with pillows stuffed under her dress, her puzzled office mates asked her what holiday she was supposed to be representing.

She responded, "Labor Day!"

5

Work Less, Play More, Earn More

All working people have heard that we're supposed to work smarter, not harder, but what, exactly, does that mean? How, exactly, do we do that?

One important step to working smarter is to learn the skills of treating work as a game. The paradox of this approach is that by working less and playing more, you will actually become more efficient and more productive. You will be better able to handle stress on the job, to reenergize yourself after a demanding project, to deal with problem situations, and to be nourished by your home life in a way that supports your work life. You will become a more valuable team member and one who is less likely to suffer from job burnout. By learning to play with the problem situations that arise on the job, you will work smarter, produce more, and earn more.

In *Managing to Have Fun,* I told a story about Kirt

Womack, who works at the Thiokol plant in Utah, which makes the booster rockets for the space shuttle. When Kirt suggested to his manager that the factory celebrate the first day of spring with a paper-airplane-flying contest, his manager was completely resistant to the idea. But when Kirt guaranteed that his shift would reach 150 percent of its daily production quota by two-thirty in the afternoon if they could have a paper-airplane-flying contest as a reward, his manager relented.

On the big day, as Kirt had predicted, his shift had reached 110 percent of its daily production quota by one-thirty in the afternoon and had reached 210 percent of its quota by two-thirty. They all celebrated by going outside and jubilantly flying their paper airplanes, and when Kirt asked his manager what he thought of their accomplishment, his manager churlishly replied, "If you can produce this well with an hour off, imagine how much more you could get done if you actually worked that hard for the whole shift!"

Wrong. A more valid observation would have been "If you can produce this well with an hour off, imagine how much *less* you could get done if you actually worked that hard for the whole shift!" Because it was obviously not *in spite of having the hour off* to play that Kirt's team produced so well, it was *because of having the hour off.* Taking the time off to play on the job with their coworkers had obvious benefits for Kirt's team. It reenergized them, made them feel rewarded, bonded them. It gave them a chance to celebrate their success and a structured opportunity to get rid of stress and tension. And, in an odd way, the fun break was not entirely unrelated to their jobs. "After all," says Kirt, "we work in the aerospace industry, so we ought to be pretty good at making paper airplanes too!"

Kirt was disappointed by his manager's skepticism but undeterred in his campaign to bring fun to work. The following week he proposed that he be allowed to bring in a volleyball net and set it up on the factory floor if his shift once again beat its quota. After the team handily trounced its quota once again that day, it began to dawn on Kirt's supervisor that the days with the highest productivity were the days when Kirt's team was having some organized fun together. So the following week when Kirt proposed that if the team once again were to beat its quota, then the manager would take them out for some ice cream, all the bemused manager could say was "Will that be chocolate or vanilla?"

As Kirt recounted this story to me, he was roaming about the factory floor on a portable phone. "I've taught everybody your idea of giving each other standing ovations," he confided. "In fact, I just walked by somebody's computer that has the words 'I want a standing ovation!' for a screen saver. Listen to this." And he bellowed out, "I WANT A STANDING OVA-TION, RIGHT NOW!" Instantly I heard a huge roar of cheering and applause in the background. "Did you hear that?" he asked me delightedly. "They don't know I'm talking to you. I could be talking to anybody!"

Is a workplace like Kirt's, which is energized and enthusiastic, where the employees have permission to openly applaud one another's successes, likely to be more productive? Of course it is. A new motto for the twenty-first-century employee might well be, Be funny, make money. There is a direct correlation between having fun on the job and being more productive.

More and more, successful companies are learning to hire, reward, and promote individuals who bring a sense of play to their work. Writing about Southwest Airlines, number one on its list of the 100 best companies to work for, *Fortune* magazine notes that the company "gets 150,000 resumes a year, yet hires just 5,000, an admissions policy that's Ivy League stingy. A sense of humor is a very serious requirement. If a candidate seems particularly taciturn, the interviewer may go for the jugular, demanding, 'Tell me a joke.' Even candidates in such mirth-deficient disciplines as finance and infotech are required to mesh with the company's famously jocular culture."

Like Southwest, Sprint knows that prospective employees will want to work for a company that has fun. To promote the opening of its Portland, Oregon, sales office, Sprint sponsored a toll-free hot line, 1-888 FUN SELL, to offer information about its philosophy of fun at work. "It's our job to be in a good mood all the time," says Tony Seelza, who manages the inside sales group for Portland. "Attitudes are contagious. We all have to ask ourselves one question when we walk through the door every morning: 'Is mine worth catching?' "

The upper management at EDS knows that if the organization is going to establish a positive employee morale, then the top-ranking executives need to model the theme of fun at work. So for International Fun at Work Day, the Southern California offices of the EDS Xerox account held a lottery, with one winner in each office. The prize? The regional vice president traveled from office to office that day, and for one hour in each location he served as a personal assistant to each of the prize-winners. Demonstrating once again that when it comes to fun at work, the three best ways to lead are by example, by example, and by example.

Some companies have taken their commitment to fun at work a step further, even making the difficult decision to fire managers who are subverting the playful corporate culture. At McGuffey's Restaurants, a thirteen-unit Southeast chain, employees evaluate how much fun a manager is to work with, which can affect 20 percent of the manager's raise. "When we're ready to promote, we ask employees, who would you want to work for?" reports McGuffey's president Keith Dunn, in an interview with *The Wall Street Journal.*

McGuffey's fired its second-highest-producing manager because he terrorized employees. Mr. Dunn explains, "We're in a business with high turnover; it's part of a manager's job to bring fun to the workplace." Management by intimidation may produce profitable results in the short term, but as Keith Dunn knows too well, it can be disastrous to the long-term economic well-being of the organization, creating the kind of oppressive corporate culture where key employees are searching for ways to escape to another company.

Organizations that incorporate an underlying philosophy of fun at work, however, are able to increase both productivity and profitability, while retaining key employees for the long run. These companies have found that a workplace that is filled with wrinkled brows does not necessarily lead to a profitable bottom line. In fact, the opposite is often true: one important benefit many managers are discovering about fun at work is that it helps them to retain their most valued employees. As the competition to retain these workers becomes more intense, managers need to treat their best employees as "volunteers," as people who could leave at any time to work somewhere else.

Successful organizations are learning to create a corporate culture where fun and play are integrated into the workplace. "Our goal is to keep people so busy having fun every day that they don't even listen when the headhunters call," says Ken Alvares, head of worldwide human resources at Sun Microsystems. And this approach is working: Sun's turnover, at 11.6 percent, is about two thirds lower than the competition's.

The employees who bring a sense of fun and celebration to their workplace may look like they work less and play more, but ultimately, they earn more too. That is because they don't really work less, they just work smarter. Theirs is a workplace that is filled with joy and energy. And the increased productivity that results is the ultimate benefit for the managers who support their employees in putting fun to work.

6

Have Fun
with Your Customers

When it comes to customer service, all business is show business, because the more fun you have with your customers, the more likely they are to continue to do business with you. "Once I get them in the store, I'm going to have a customer for a long time, because our store environment is such fun they're going to want to come back over and over again," says Dick Snow of Ben & Jerry's ice cream. "We believe that we're in the entertainment business, and selling ice cream is just a part of what we do. In our store the counter is our stage, and the customers are our audience."

After you have created an enticing atmosphere at your place of business, the next step is to dream up some inventive ways to let prospective customers know about your fun-friendly environment. Lynn McDonald, another Ben & Jerry's franchisee, printed up prescription pads, which she distributed to the pediatricians in her town.

After each visit, the doctors could reward their youthful patients with a prescription for a free ice-cream cone from Ben & Jerry's. And of course these youthful customers brought their parents along with them, simultaneously introducing the whole family to the joys of Ben & Jerry's.

In another marketing masterstroke, Lynn printed up "I know who you are, and I saw what you did" tickets, which she distributed to local police officers. The police would give these tickets to people they caught performing "random acts of kindness"; each ticket was good for a free ice-cream cone. This not only promoted Lynn's business to people in the community, it also gave her a chance to reward the citizens of her hometown of Sarasota, Florida, for their good deeds.

Jerry Greenfield, one of the founders of Ben & Jerry's, is famous for his motto "If it's not fun, why do it?" So it isn't surprising that so many Ben & Jerry's franchisees have found creative ways to let their customers interact with their employees. At Judy Goodale's scoop shop in Cape Cod, every Tuesday night became theme night—Mexican Night, Seventies Night, or Hawaiian Night. The scoopers dressed up in costume and played music that reflected the theme all night long, and any customers who came to the store dressed up in costume got a free topping on their ice cream.

And once the customers entered the store, there were numerous spontaneous contests, like free cones for anyone who could do the "YMCA" dance when the song was playing, or free cones for anyone who could sing the lyrics to a song louder than the song was playing. Or the ever-popular "If you moo like a cow when you enter the store, you get free sprinkles" ("Which not only gives the employees a laugh whenever it happens," comments Susan Bowman, Ben & Jerry's director of franchise operations, "it is also a really good way for us to identify our regular customers").

One of Ben & Jerry's signature flavors is called Chubby

Hubby. So Lynn McDonald set up a Chubby Hubby Contest, with a free Chubby Hubby cone for the woman with the chubbiest hubby. When I expressed my doubts that women would want to go public with their husbands' chubbiness, she laughed and said, "Never underestimate the power of a free ice-cream cone! Most of the time as soon as we announce the contest, we have women who pull open their husbands' shirts to show that their big beer bellies are real and then push them to the front of the line to collect their prize."

You don't have to be part of a large organization like Ben & Jerry's to have fun with your customers. Taxicab driver Toni Guglielmi drives an impeccably restored 1965 Checker Cab. Her company, Bay Area Checker, is a one-person operation. Toni has been so successful in garnering a large following of loyal customers all over the San Francisco metropolitan area that she never has to advertise her services. In fact, she only accepts new customers if they are referred to her by other customers. "I'm in the fortunate position that I don't need to be trolling the streets for a fare," says Toni. "I can afford to be selective about who I'll take on as a customer. In fact, my motto about new customers is, 'If I don't want you, you can't have me!' "

To thank her customers for their ongoing support and referrals, Toni created a Customer Appreciation Day. One afternoon she rented out her favorite Italian restaurant and threw a party for all her regular customers, complete with free food and drink, speeches, toasts, and songs.

"Some of the most interesting people in the Bay Area are customers of mine," says Toni. "They've been hearing about each other from me for years. So I figured I might as well gather them all in one place, thank them for their support, and let them all finally meet each other in the flesh!"

Many successful companies are well known for "relationship selling." Successful salespeople at these companies know that the intentional use of laughter, play, and fun can help to distinguish them from their competition and establish a good feeling between themselves and prospective customers. Brian Palmer, vice president of the National Speakers' Bureau, recalls a time that he had a good working relationship with a client at a large investment firm. There was another executive in the firm, at a higher level, with whom Brian did not do much business. Brian asked his client about this, and she told him that her boss had told her jokingly, "Brian doesn't suck up nearly enough." His client assured Brian that this was intended as some sort of a compliment, because her boss delivered this comment with good humor.

Brian had purchased a new Dustbuster portable vacuum cleaner for his home the previous day, and instead he immediately sent it off to his client's boss.

"I don't get it," I told Brian. "What was that supposed to do?"

"Oh, well, I also sent a letter along with it," he explained. "It said, 'Since I can't be there, I send the enclosed to do my sucking up for me!'

"I'm told that he came close to falling off his chair when he opened the package. I also heard that he walked around the office showing his gift to all his underlings as a great example of 'sucking up.' "

On the one-year anniversary of this gift, Brian sent the executive a package of replacement filters. "It turned out in the end that he did not have very much business to give, after all," concludes Brian. "Though what he had, he gave to me."

Of course, Brian's special technique might be inappropriate for your own particular style of doing business, but his basic approach is a valuable one—do something fun to create a relationship with your clients that sets you apart from your competitors. How about sending your top prospect a surprise pizza, with your phone number spelled out across the top of the pie, in mushrooms!

7

If You Haven't Been Rejected Recently, Then You Probably Haven't Been Trying Hard Enough

I see my job in this book as similar to that of a champion chicken sexer. For those few of you who may never have crossed paths with a professional chicken sexer, let me explain that little-known career alternative.

When baby chicks are hatched it is almost impossible to determine their sex. Only a skilled chicken sexer can accurately identify which are to be roosters and which are to be hens. There is no easy path to becoming a chicken sexer, no simple rules to follow, no correspondence course that can be taken, no how-to books. The only way to do it is to stand next to a professional chicken sexer and watch. Then you try it yourself, until you catch on.

Becoming a more playful person is in many ways like becoming a professional chicken sexer. In this book I will ask you to "stand next to" a number of playful individuals, and then to try it yourself, in your own way.

One such person is Ellie Katz, a nurse whose motto is Be outrageous—it's the only place left that's not crowded! When Ellie visits a friend in the hospital, she never brings flowers, candy, or presents. When other visitors ask her if she has brought along any gifts, she gives them a conspiratorial smile. "Gifts?" she asks. "Of course I brought a gift. I *am* the gift!" This seems to me a wonderful way of thinking about yourself, one that can be a powerful tool for every one of us. The most positive, playful stance to take in dealing with other people is to realize that you have a gift to share with them and that, in fact, *that gift is you.*

This attitude can be a great asset in the business world as well. Sales managers are constantly on the lookout for a way to predict which of their many job applicants will turn into successful salespeople and which will not. If there is one factor that seems to consistently predict the ability to handle the day-to-day rejection that comes with any sales job, it is high self-esteem—the inner knowledge that you are, in fact, a gift.

The better you feel about yourself, the less likely you are to take yourself too seriously, and the more you are able to laugh at yourself and the things that may go wrong all around you. People with high self-esteem feel good about themselves from the inside out; their moods are not dependent on what happens to them in the outside world. When they get rejected on a sales call, they don't take it personally. Because they have the attitude that they are a gift, they uplift the people around them. And since sales is an emotional, relationship-centered business, it is no surprise that they make a lot of sales and a lot of money.

Of course, you don't need to be a salesperson to experience rejection—all of us experience some form of rejection in our lives. Once you learn to ask for what you want, you also learn that you won't always get it. But you certainly won't get what you want if you never even ask for it. That is why every successful businessperson has a history of rejection. In fact, if you haven't been rejected recently, then you probably haven't been trying hard enough. You haven't been taking enough risks or asking for what you want.

If you can adopt the attitude that you are a gift, then you will be much better equipped to deal with ups and downs, to accept that rejection is an everyday fact of life. I first discovered this principle in action several years ago when I went out to a nightclub in Massachusetts with my friend Eddie. We were sitting at the bar having a couple of beers when Eddie became fascinated by a woman dancing alone in the middle of the dance floor. He was very attracted to her and he kept looking at her and talking about her. So I said to him, "Well, why don't you go dance with her, then?" No, he said, he didn't feel like dancing.

Finally, after a couple more tall mugs of courage, he suddenly got up from his bar stool, gave me a wink, and went over to the dance floor. He walked up to the woman, gave her a big smile, and said, "Excuse me, would you like to dance?"

She stopped dancing for a brief moment, gave him a cold look of contempt, and said, "I'm *already* dancing!"

Eddie was truly mortified. He walked off the dance floor and right out of the nightclub, and I didn't see him again for the rest of the week. When I finally did see him, I tried to bring the incident up in a lighthearted way. "Hey, Eddie," I said with a grin, "do you remember that strange woman dancing at the bar the other night?"

He turned to me with an intense glimmer in his eye. "Do I remember her?" he asked. "I've been in therapy over that incident for the entire week!" Then he assured me that he had it all handled. "I have replayed that episode in my mind enough times so that now I understand exactly what I should have done."

"Oh, really?" I was intrigued. "What's that?"

"Well, I go over to this woman and I say to her, 'Hey, would you like to dance?' And she says to me, 'I'm *already* dancing!' And so I slowly look her up and down, and finally I say to her, 'You call that *dancing*?' "

The perfect comeback, only a week too late.

And yet, of course, it was not the perfect comeback—it was merely an excellent example of being reactive. Whenever you feel attacked and you immediately defend yourself with an un-thinking counterattack, then you have entered the reacting state of mind. And in that mode, you invariably cut yourself off from any possibility of finding laughter and joy in the present moment. You forget that you are a gift with something valuable to offer the other person; instead you feel as if you are fighting for your life.

If I insult you and then you insult me back, you are reacting to me. You are not in control of your behavior—I am. You are not choosing to live your own life, you are merely responding to whatever stimulus comes your way. A reaction to a negative sit-uation will always be negative itself. In fact the word *reactionary* describes someone who is hostile toward change and progress. Reacting is always a dead end.

When we react to rejection with a hostile counterattack, it is because some part of us actually believes that we deserve to be rejected. Some part of us believes that we are unworthy at the core, and so we need to ferociously defend ourselves from letting the "truth" about ourselves be known. But let's imagine that someone insults you by telling you that you look like a Martian. You wouldn't get defensive or reactive—you'd just look at him like he's lost his mind. You'd probably burst out laughing. Because you know it isn't true.

When you feel good about yourself internally, then nothing that anyone else says can make you feel reactive. Anytime someone makes an unprovoked, hostile remark to you, you know

it is usually an expression of his own insecurity, her own inade-
quacies. You don't need to respond to the attack by asking yourself, "What's wrong with me?" and then proceeding to defend
yourself. Instead, you can ask yourself, "What's wrong with
him?" You realize that your attacker is out of touch with his own
sense of self-worth.

One of the most positive ways to regard an off-the-wall attack, insult, or rejection is with understanding, empathy, and
pity for your attacker. It tells you more about that person than
it tells you about yourself.

Anytime you ask for something you want, anytime you take
a risk, you set yourself up for the possibility of rejection. If you
can think of yourself as a gift, it is much easier to respond to
such a rejection with compassion and to say to yourself, "Hey, if
this person doesn't want to take the time to unwrap the package and check out the gift, that's her problem, not mine. It
doesn't make me any less valuable a present."

8

Take the Company on a Shopping Spree

Most people spend more time working, commuting to work, and thinking about work than they do all of their other waking activities combined. So if you're not having fun at work, you'll wind up being fun-deprived for the majority of your waking life. Even one small step toward bringing fun to work can have a profound effect on the way a company does business.

Mike Phillips is the owner of the Migra Textiles mill in Cape Town, South Africa. For the tenth anniversary of his company, Mike designed a special celebration to reward his employees for their years of hard work. Inspired by a story he read in *Managing to Have Fun,* Mike put all his employees on board a bus for a "magical mystery tour." The bus deposited them at a fancy shopping mall, where Mike gave each of his employees the equivalent of two hundred dollars in South African currency. He then told them,

"You have one hour to spend all this money on presents for yourself. You have to buy at least five different things, and if there is any money unspent after an hour, you have to give it all back to me. Any questions? See you in an hour!"

Mike reported that his employees had so much fun that the store clerks were asking them, "What company do you work for? I've got to quit my job and start working there!"

One of Mike's custodial employees had started buying gifts for all her children with the bonus money. The other Migra employees made her put all the gifts back and forced her instead to buy a leather jacket for herself. It was the first luxury item she had ever purchased for her own use in her entire life.

In the middle of this companywide shopping spree, the union shop steward came up to Mike, all smiles, and confided to him, "If you're going to keep treating us like this, then we're going to have to look at you a little bit differently from now on!" The next month there was a national strike of all the textile mills in South Africa, and only one of them did not participate: Migra Textiles. Mike attributes this fact entirely to the change in attitude that took place between union and management from that one-day celebration, when all the employees went out to play together on the company shopping spree.

Your own position in the organization may not enable you to authorize a companywide shopping spree. On the other hand, every individual, regardless of his job description, can do something to make the work environment a more playful, nourishing one. So the real question you need to ask yourself is "How can I find a way to translate the spirit of the company shopping spree into my own work situation, as a gift to myself and my coworkers?"

Playfair Vice Emperor Ritch Davidson and Vice Empress Terry Sand once dreamed up an inexpensive alternative to the company shopping spree, one that had a similar impact on their coworkers. They asked everyone in the company to bring a pair of old shoes in to work. They had to be shoes that still fit us but that we didn't wear anymore and that we were willing to donate to the company.

Terry visited her local crafts-supply store and offered to buy all the supplies that fell on the floor during the course of the day, which the store would normally throw away. For five dollars a bag, she acquired mounds of artificial flowers, Styrofoam ornaments, and exotic fabrics. Ritch, meanwhile, purchased a wide variety of plastic animals, rubber insects and fish, plastic eyeballs, mirrored hearts, and assorted sparkles, sequins, and glitter.

Ritch and Terry also provided plenty of spray paint and hot-glue guns, and we all went to work decorating one another's shoes with these unusual ornaments. The rule was that every two minutes each person each had to move on to another shoe, so that everyone got to make a contribution to every single shoe. When these magnificent items of wearable art were finally completed, we wore them the next day as part of a tribute to one of our trainers, who was celebrating his twentieth year of service to the company. It was a priceless moment in Playfair history as the entire company stood gathered outdoors in a circle, beaming proudly at one another as our shoes glittered in the sunlight and called out to us, "It's time for fun!"

The shoes were then put on permanent display in the conference room at the Playfair office, where they remain to this day. They always provide a wonderful conversational ice-breaker whenever we have client meetings at our offices. And occasionally, in the middle of an otherwise serious staff meeting, someone will demand, "Let's put on our shoes!" The tenor of the meeting immediately lightens up as we are instantly flooded with memories of creating the shoes together—a time of heightened playfulness and creativity for everyone who participated.

Like the Migra Textiles shopping spree that helped the mill avoid a general strike, Terry and Ritch's shoe-design festival created some shared history for their coworkers, which let them see one another in a different light from the one in which they ordinarily view one another during the working day. How can one small act of play make such a huge difference at work? The language of play is a powerful one, one that we all speak in common. It is the language of connection and of joy. It is the language that speaks eloquently of the universal dream that every working person shares—to work and thrive in a supportive community where we find ourselves valued, celebrated, and appreciated.

9

Work Like
Your Dog

The employees of the Brookline Booksmith have found an unusual way to bond with their customers: through their customers' dogs. The bookstore employees always have dog biscuits on hand for visiting canines, and they try to learn the names of all their customers' pets. In the heat of the summer, the bookstore, which was voted the most dog-friendly store in Boston by the readers of *Boston* magazine, has a watercooler outside its front entrance for thirsty pedestrians as well as a bowser bowl of water for any dogs who may be passing by.

Each month the bookstore features a "Dog of Distinction" in its newsletter. In addition to running a photo of the chosen pooch, the article profiles its pet peeves, listing the dog's "turn-ons" like "bags of bagels, birthday cake, and shoes" and "turn-offs," like "eating too little and walking too fast." "Of course, people send us all kinds of pictures of their pets, not only their dogs, but their birds, their cats, whatever," says Dana Brigham, the store manager. "One month we actually ran a photo of a cat for our Dog of Distinction, just to see if anyone was paying attention!"

One of the most popular times of the year for both customers and employees of the Brookline Booksmith is the Dog Days of August. During that month, the store window features the hundreds of dog photos that have been submitted during the year for the Dog of Distinction. The books featured in the window all have a canine theme as well, like Charles Bukowski's *Love Is a Dog from Hell*, David Hockney's *Dog Days*, and Russell Banks's *Rule of the Bone*. "Our customers love to point out the photos of their dogs in the window to each other," Dana recounts. "One of our missions is to introduce people to books they wouldn't ordinarily find on their own, and the Dog Days of August gives our employees one more chance to put a personal spin on the books they recommend to our customers."

Of course, it should come as no surprise that the employees of the Brookline Booksmith have been able to enhance their business practices by spending time in the company of dogs. The idea of associating dogs with work has a long history. How many times have you heard people complain that they've been "working like a dog"? Or perhaps you've heard people say that if you want to get ahead at work, the key is to "work like a dog." The idea is that if we want to be successful, then we must be prepared to work long hours at hard labor. Working like a dog will most likely be a tiresome, serious, and joyless affair, without a hint of laughter, fun, or play.

However, before you ever use the phrase "work like a dog" again, take a moment to think about how your own dog actually spends her days. I wonder if the people using the phrase "work like a dog" have ever had a meaningful relationship with a real dog. For that matter, I wonder if they know any real dogs at all.

I think comedian George Carlin demonstrated a much better understanding of a dog's life when he posed the question "Have you ever wondered what a dog does on his day off?" The only reason that this question strikes us as funny is because most of us have a pretty clear idea that a dog's life truly blurs the distinction between work and play.

In fact, I am ready to say without hesitation that if you *really* want to be successful, if you *really* want to get ahead, and if you *really* want to be happy in your job, then you have to learn to work like a dog. I hasten to add, however, that you must be very clear about how most dogs go about their work.

As a model of the working dog, I propose that we take a look at my own dog, Blue. When my wife selected Blue, the only female in a litter of seven, the breeders provided her with the following caution: "She's not really a golden retriever who has show dogs in her pedigree. She comes from the finest breed of field retrievers. She's a working dog, and she's going to need lots of work."

I wasn't in the least concerned about this warning. As an avid long-distance runner, I wanted a golden retriever partly as a running companion. I figured that the eight to ten miles of running that I was doing each day should be enough work for her. If not, I knew I could always get her a second job retrieving Frisbees and tennis balls. Now, after more than six years of closely observing Blue, I can offer a few examples of how a working dog works.

As soon as Blue notices that I'm getting dressed for a run, she does not let me out of her sight. When she sees the running shoes being pulled from the closet she gets so excited that she literally leaps in the air, with all four feet leaving the ground. A huge smile lights up her face as she springs toward the door. How many people do you know who show that kind of enthusiasm for going to work in the morning?

Blue has the decided advantage of being a much faster runner than her human running partner. As a result, she finds many opportunities during our run to integrate play into her work. As we do our morning loop around the lake by our house, she nearly always finds time to fit in a swim or two. Every squirrel spotting calls for a playful chase. Her workday is a fine example of curiosity in action. She takes a joyful break to wallow in any mud she can find. She also takes time from her work to stop and say hello to virtually every child we pass.

While it's true that she takes her work as a retriever a bit more seriously than her work as a running companion, she doesn't let her intense focus on Frisbees and balls detract from her ability to treat work as a game. Upon returning with a retrieved object, she will respond to a sharply worded command, *"Drop!"* However, she very much prefers—before you give the command—to place the object immediately within your reach, and then engage you for a few minutes in a game of keep-away or tug-of-war before the next toss. She also demonstrates another very positive work ethic—consideration and sensitivity—by modifying her game when she is retrieving for young children. She rushes back with a retrieved ball, stops a few feet away so as to avoid startling the child, and then places the ball on the ground before gently nudging it to the child with her nose. Children squeal with delight.

Of course, not every part of Blue's workday is all that perfect or positive. Like most golden retrievers, she rarely passes up an opportunity to roll around in cow poop, dead fish, or any other disgusting matter she can find. (Many of us can relate to this kind of experience in our own workday. You probably have had a similar feeling of being covered in cow poop countless times as you walked away from a particularly difficult meeting.) On today's run, for example, Blue was caught in a torrent of filthy water rushing through a drainpipe, and she spent quite a bit of time wandering around looking like a drowned rat. However, she doesn't let these little setbacks and digressions ruin her day. She puts the negative stuff behind her and gets on with her work.

Integrating our lives as parents with our lives as working people can be difficult for most of us, and Blue was no different in this respect. I remember so well the night she delivered her only litter of puppies. She had a very large litter, even for a golden retriever. As soon as she had delivered her thirteenth beautiful, healthy golden pup, she stood up, stepped out of the whelping box, ran to get her Frisbee, and then bolted out into the backyard. She would not be comforted and return to her pups until I very reluctantly agreed to toss the Frisbee at least once. I am convinced that this was her way of communicating to me that although she now might be the mother of thirteen, our life together of work and play wasn't about to change. She was a wonderful mother, but as soon as the pups were weaned, it was back to work as usual—meaning fun, fun, fun.

There are many dogs, of course, who have much more important and serious jobs than Blue does. Over the years I have been fortunate to know a variety of dogs who work as Seeing Eye guides, household helpers, and rescue dogs. They are dedicated companions who do invaluable work, and they approach their work with the same spirit, enthusiasm, and joy as does Blue. They all seem to know that work and play do not have to be mutually exclusive.

Nearly all working dogs—whether it's Blue or a rescue dog working the ski slopes—are great models for us to emulate in our own work lives. They approach their work not only with dedication, loyalty, discipline, sensitivity, and love, but also with joy, enthusiasm, and happiness. If you want to increase your abilities in this area of study, spend a few hours this week in the company of a dog. The first thing you will notice is that the dog is constantly living in the present moment. Everything is of interest to her: the sights, the smells, the slightest movement in the world around her. Nothing seems boring; every interaction with another being brings its own excitement. So many things bring her pleasure. Notice how good you feel around her, how you are filled with joy, tenderness, concentrated focus, and excitement. Notice how she makes you laugh, over and over again.

That is exactly how other people can feel in your presence, as well, once you learn to go on out there and work like a dog.

10

Honor Your Fabulous Failures

If a business is to innovate and grow, then its employees need to constantly experiment with doing things differently than they've always been done. Which means that a successful business venture needs to support its employees to take risks and to fail, as well as to succeed.

"For me, one of the keys to creating an atmosphere at work where people feel free to have fun and to experiment," says Lynne Mattone, Hawaii-based sales manager for Lucent Technologies, "is that you don't come down on people for their mistakes. If I'm going to encourage my people to be asking questions, to be finding out for themselves how this business works, to be discovering new solutions for old problems, then there's no such thing as a stupid question."

When Lucent held its President's Club award meeting in Hawaii, Lynne was asked to serve as the guide on a bus tour of the island for the award winners. So she grabbed the microphone and regaled her colleagues with an ongoing commentary on the sights the bus was passing by, including whatever fractured history of the island she could conjure up from her school days. Finally, after she had exhausted her dim memory of the highlights of island history, Lynne asked if there were any questions.

"Yes," replied one of the women on board, raising her hand enthusiastically. "Is there water *all around* the island?"

"I have to say," Lynne says, laughing, "that like anybody else I was immediately tempted to answer, 'Yes, pinhead, of course there is water all the way around the island—*that's why they call it an island!*' But what good does it ever do to make fun of somebody's stupid questions? It just makes everyone else paranoid about asking questions in the future, and of looking stupid themselves. So instead I just said, 'Well, do you know what, we're going to be driving all the way around the island. Why don't we just wait and see!' "

David Robertson, CEO of Duncan Regional Hospital in Duncan, Oklahoma, found an even stronger way to support his employees in taking risks and learning to fail with panache. David holds a monthly "lunch with the CEO" for some of his employees, and as he was walking through the cafeteria line in preparation for one of those luncheons, he came to the butter basket, which was empty. When he sat down to lunch with the hospital employees, he asked if any of them had noticed the empty butter basket, and all of them had. But none of them had said anything about it to the cafeteria staff.

"Isn't it interesting," David commented, "that all of us would rather just go along with the status quo, and not make waves, than point out an area in which the cafeteria needs to improve. And I bet that's true of the rest of our departments as well. We hide our failures behind closed doors, instead of holding them up to the light of day where we can improve upon our mistakes."

Out of that luncheon came the quarterly Butter Basket Award, which goes to the hospital employee who has learned the most from a fabulous failure. The award is an actual basket filled with several hundred dollars' worth of gourmet foods. But more important, says David, is the message it conveys: "When we celebrate our fabulous failures, we increase our chances to have fabulous successes."

Those of us who spend our professional lives giving speeches get instantaneous feedback from our audiences about the success or failure of our work. At a Playfair staff meeting, I reminded the assembled trainers that if we were committed to constantly trying out new things with our clients, then we were undoubtedly going to experiment with some things that didn't work out so well. So we discussed the possibility of finding something positive in our inevitable failures. Al Pollo, one of the Playfair trainers, told us about a time he had given a presentation to a convention of more than seven hundred people. When he finished his address, Al was very gratified to receive a thunderous standing ovation, and afterward a number of people came over to talk with him. One gentleman asked if he could speak to Al privately.

"I thought that he must have some personal question and wanted some of my sage advice," Al confided. "So I excused myself from the others, so that we could have a few minutes in private. Once he had me alone he said, 'You know, this is the third time I've heard you speak, and actually you are pretty good. There is one problem, however. When you first start off your speeches you say "uh" quite a bit. After you've been going for a while, you stop doing it. I suggest that you get with a good speech teacher who could help you with that problem.'

"I felt horrible," moaned Al. "For the rest of the evening, all I could think of was that one critical voice, telling me that I was a failure. I was totally unable to enjoy the success of my presentation, because I was focused on that one negative response. It took me quite a while to get things more into perspective. Most of the people, after all, had been able to overlook my 'failure' and enjoy the presentation quite a bit.

"We'll always have critics who don't like what we do, whatever it is. If we have to wait until we are one hundred percent perfect before we can feel successful, then our wait will never end! So I've tried very hard to give more of my attention to the positive voices and less to the negative ones. On the other hand, I actually did speak with a speech teacher about what she called my 'verbalizing pauses.' With her help, I have almost completely changed the habit of saying 'uh' whenever I pause. So in the end, I was really grateful for that man's advice, even though it knocked me for a loop."

As a manager, I have found that supporting the members of my team through their small failures can ultimately lead to huge successes for the organization. Fran Solomon is the senior vice empress of Playfair and one of the world's leading authorities on fun at work. After ten years of traveling the world delivering corporate trainings on "Managing to Have Fun," Fran came to me one time and confessed that she felt like she was losing her edge. "I just don't have the passion for the work that I used to have," she explained. "I feel like I've said it all and done it all before."

Fran had been a professional musician before joining the Playfair organization, and she had always kept up her interest in music. In fact, she had just released a CD of original songs, called *Woman in the Moon,* and she had recently given a series of concerts. "I feel like when I am onstage singing my songs, I can let my authentic self come out. I used to feel that same way about the Managing to Have Fun programs," she lamented, "but I can't seem to get to that place in my corporate lectures anymore."

"Okay," I proposed. "Then why don't you start singing some of your songs as part of your corporate lectures?"

"Sing my songs to corporate audiences?" she asked, surprised.

"Sure, why not?" I replied. I was a big fan of Fran's songs, and I knew her CD inside out. In fact, the more I thought about it, the more I really liked the idea. I enthusiastically suggested that her songs, like "Magic" and "Partners in Pride," might be an inspiration to the people in her audience who were struggling to build a team and who were having difficulty believing in their own abilities to succeed.

Fran excitedly agreed to give it a shot, and I eagerly awaited the results. I didn't have long to wait. Fran was scheduled to give a presentation that week to the American Nurses Association, and we had planned a debriefing meeting for the next day.

"So, how did it go?" I asked her.

"Oh, it went great," she replied offhandedly. "I got a big standing ovation."

"That's wonderful! And the song?"

Here she dejectedly flipped a sheet of paper across the table to me. It was a participant evaluation form, and as I started to read through it Fran pointed to the comments section. In large block letters, it read, CUT THE SONG!

"Ouch!" I said. "And did anyone else write anything positive about the song?"

"Oh, sure," she replied. "In fact a bunch of people really liked it."

"That's great! So what are you going to do?"

"What am I going to do? I'm going to cut the song!"

"Oh, no, you're not going to cut the song. That's just one person's opinion. But here's my opinion. You're going to keep singing a song in every one of your presentations from now on. In fact, your new motto is going to be Don't sit down until you sing!"

Here Fran began to laugh. "I don't sit down until I've sung? Those are your instructions to me?"

"Those are my instructions to you!"

Fran has followed those instructions to the letter. Her songs have become a signature component of all her presentations. And from that day forward, almost every time she has finished a song, her audience has leaped to its feet to interrupt her presentation with a standing ovation.

Fran tells the "cut the song" story to her audiences, as an example of how all of us tend to listen more to negative voices than to positive ones. And of how we often will need to pass through some failure to get to our ultimate success.

—11—

Value Who You Are, Not What You Have

How many times have you heard someone say, "I'm just a secretary," or "I'm only a clerk in the mailroom"? And just as frequently we hear someone say with a tad too much hubris, "I'm the CEO," or "I own this company."

These days so many of us, especially in the United States, seem confused about the value we place on job titles or job descriptions. This confusion can lead us into two possible mistakes. We can get mired in low self-esteem and think that we are less valuable than other people because of our failure to get a big bonus or that longed-for promotion; or, when we finally do achieve a certain measure of success, we can get puffed up with self-importance. Both mistakes stand in the way of a joyful work life that is filled with laughter and play. In both cases, we are taking ourselves far too seriously; we are focusing too much on what we do and not enough on who we are.

The ancient philosopher Socrates spent much of his life trying to teach that all things that are truly good flow from having achieved human excellence—that is, from having nourished and developed our character as human beings. According to Socrates, it doesn't really matter if we have achieved wealth, fame, or a position of leadership if we have not first become the right kind of person. He thought it better to be the poor servant of a poor master than to live a life in which we are deluded into thinking that our job title, our money, our material possessions, or our fame somehow make us better people. At some level, we all know that Socrates was right; but we still too easily get caught up in mistaken symbols of success—job titles, salaries, schooling, and other trappings that express nothing of our true character.

For much of human history, there has been no greater erroneous symbol of success than one's mode of transportation. The ricksha, the royal palanquin, the carriage and four, the company stretch limo—all of these have been supposed to reflect something about their occupant's place in the world. I remember quite clearly the day that the extent of this problem was revealed to me. I was leading a discussion about the German philosopher Feuerbach, who once wrote, *"Man ist, was man isst"*—a man is what he eats. After a brief discussion about what Feuerbach may have had in mind, a young man slouched in the back row with his feet hanging between the rows of seats bellowed, "WRONG!" In true Socratic fashion, I allowed that, indeed, Feuerbach might have been wrong, then I asked the young man to explain why. With great confidence he said, "Because a *man* is what he *drives*!"

This response was particularly unsettling to me, because of the vehicle I was driving at the time. For several years, before I decided it was an excellent way to get myself killed, I traveled to work every day by moped, a mode of transportation that my students usually viewed as infinitely worse than a bicycle. After all, as one of my male students once said to me, "Only wimps drive mopeds." It *is* hard to feel like a macho man on a moped. Several times when I was stuck in traffic, I would get the urge to throw my moped over my shoulder and walk home with it.

The moped is anathema to my male students because our social values subtly teach them that their manhood is associated with the kind of car they drive. The message is "Don't value who you are, value what you have." The futility of this point of view was demonstrated quite dramatically to a young gentleman I once met at a red light as I was driving home, I on my moped and he in his Trans Am.

We were sitting side by side for what seemed like an interminable light, both pretending, as we humans often do at stoplights, that the other person does not exist. (After all, when you're on a moped at a stoplight, it's almost as if you're riding in the car with the person next to you.) He had his window down, and I must give him credit, for he broke the silence between us.

"How fast does that thing go?" he asked me.

"Oh, about twenty-two or twenty-three miles per hour," I replied, trying to be friendly. "Unless I'm going downhill, of course." Then I tried to save my ego a bit by adding, "But it sure gets good gas mileage. Drives right past those service stations!"

He wasn't impressed. He just pumped his accelerator two or three times and said, "Right," and drove off.

The traffic was pretty heavy that day. When I got to the street where I usually turn, about ten miles from that stoplight, I happened to look a block ahead, and there, to my amazement, was the Trans Am, stopped at the next light. Even though I was supposed to turn left, and even though I was certainly supposed to wait for my own light to turn green, I did neither. I ran the light and pulled to a stop next to the Trans Am. The driver did one of those classic double takes. I smiled at him and continued our conversation right where we had left off. "By the way," I said, "how fast does that thing go?"

"Well, I'll tell you," he replied thoughtfully, his voice filled with disgust, "obviously not fast enough!"

Anytime we worry that we're not good enough, or that there is a certain cultural standard of achievement that we have to measure up to, that we don't have an impressive-enough job title or job description, we start to worry about our self-image. And whenever we become concerned about what other people think about us, we undermine our ability to laugh at ourselves. The answer to the question "What do you do?" has come to be the way many people judge the value of an individual. Although there is certainly nothing wrong with having a "good" place in the organization, or having wealth and all the material possessions that go along with it, the more you really come to know yourself, the more you come to realize that these things are only appearances, and they don't indicate a person's true beauty. Socrates, for example, was not noted for his physical appearance, nor was he known for his job as a stonecutter. He was actually pretty ugly and didn't have any money to speak of, yet he was—(and is)—considered by many people to be the most beautiful Athenian who ever lived.

Flashier cars, bigger houses, larger bank accounts, or a higher spot on the corporate ladder don't reflect our essence as human beings or make us special people. The wise Stoic philosopher Epictetus pointed this out more than eighteen hundred years ago when he said, "These reasonings have no logical connection: I am richer than you, therefore I am your superior. I am more eloquent than you, therefore I am your superior. The true logical connection is this: I am richer than you, therefore my possessions must exceed yours. I am more eloquent than you, therefore my style must surpass yours. But you, after all, consist neither in property nor in style."

When we realize this truth, we free ourselves up to have material things if we choose to, to forgo them if we choose to. Most important, we leave ourselves free to laugh about our attachment to our material possessions when, as happens to everyone, they get stolen or broken or tarnished or outdated, or when they become more of a burden to us than we had bargained for.

12

Memo to Managers: Treat Your Employees Even Better Than You Treat Your Customers

Many successful managers have realized that the best way to create excellent customer service is through *internal* customer service: *treating your own employees even better than you expect them to treat the end customer.* Before you can ask your employees to deliver service with a smile, you first have to ask yourself, "Am I giving them anything to smile about?" Any company that wants to improve its internal customer service can begin with an innovative reward-and-recognition program and a manager who models the importance of fun at work.

One might imagine that the owners of the Ben & Jerry's scoop shops, who pride themselves on creative interactions with their customers, would be equally creative in rewarding and recognizing their employees. "We get a great many orders from local businesses for ice-cream cakes, for their employee birthday parties," says Dick

Snow. "So I've made it known throughout the community that if a business wants to order an ice-cream cake from Ben & Jerry's, they can't pay cash—they have to pay for it in gift certificates to their own store. That way it's a win-win for everybody. The cake costs them a lot less, since they're paying for it in trade, and I can then distribute the gift certificates as presents to my employees."

Similarly, Dana Brigham of the Brookline Booksmith has swapped gift certificates with local merchants in her area, so that employees of her bookstore get discounts on their purchases at Gyro's juice bar, J. P. Lick's ice-cream store, Starbucks, the Videosmith, and the Coolidge Corner Cinema, while employees of those businesses get discounts on book purchases at the Brookline Booksmith.

"I want this business to be 'corporate detox' for my employees," says Lynn McDonald of Ben & Jerry's. "So I hold staff meetings at my house, where I cook for them, and ask for their input in decision making. And at our staff meetings, I encourage the scoopers to tell stories of their toughest customers, their funniest customers, their most ridiculous customers."

Marjorie Tippin is the vice president of the inside sales centers at the Sprint business division in Dallas. One of her group objectives is called "transforming the workplace"—and a subset of that is "fun at work."

"You don't get what you don't inspect," says Marjorie, so each week she asks those who report to her to let her know, in writing, about two fun things that have happened in their areas during the week.

"The inside sales centers are all telemarketers, and the public doesn't see them. So they're able to have lots of fun with the dress codes," reports Marjorie. During the course of one year at the Portland office, for example, there was Plaid and Checkers Day, Wacky Hat Day, Dressing Up Like the Sixties and Seventies Day, and California Day (where all the employees came to work in flip-flops, beachwear, caps, and sunglasses).

The Denver office created a daily *Wheel of Fortune* contest for its employees. At the end of each workday, a volunteer spins the big wheel, which has eleven different categories on it, like "made the most sales," "made the highest total number of phone calls," or "talked to the most new prospects."

"A prize is awarded for whatever category comes up," explains Marjorie. "But you never know what's going to be rewarded on any particular day, so you have to try to excel in all those areas if you're going to win the prize. Then, the person who wins for the day spins another big wheel, which has eleven different prizes on it, like movie tickets, Blockbuster Video certificates, or free lunch for two."

"But my favorite part," Marjorie says with a laugh, "is that the next morning, Gary Chowder, the group manager, delivers your prize to you by a remote-control toy car that zips in and out of all the cubicles—until it finally stops at the winner's."

Treating your employees with a sense of fun can also help them to resolve problems with difficult customers. A bank in New York was having some ongoing difficulties with customers who always complained about the service and demanded special treatment. The tellers hated these "problem" customers, and these customers hated the tellers right back. Every time one of these customers entered the bank there was tension in the air, and the situation was escalating every day. The bank manager asked management consultant David Baum for his advice.

David suggested that the manager offer an expensive bottle of French wine to the teller who could tell the worst horror story about dealing with a problem customer at the weekly staff meeting. This inspired suggestion completely changed the way the tellers began to view their problem customers. Whenever one of these customers entered the bank, the tellers now saw a giant wine bottle with legs walking toward them. So the tellers began to fight over who would serve these customers. "Hey, Frank, how are you, buddy, come on over here, let me help you out. No, no, come on over here—hey, Sandra, I saw him first!"

As David suspected might happen, once the customers were treated better, they in turn developed a more appreciative attitude toward the bank and its employees. By using a fun gimmick to break the ongoing cycle of hostility, David's intervention was able to clear the air and let the tellers and their customers conduct their relationship on new footing.

When you reward your internal customers, you indirectly reward your external customers as well. This is one instance where the trickle-down theory of economics actually works.

13

Five Unusual Ways
to Have Fun
at Work

"Fun is not frivolous anymore, if it ever was," concludes *Fortune* magazine in a cover story entitled "The 100 Best Companies to Work For." *Fortune* reports that Interim Services, a Fort Lauderdale–based temporary-staffing company, and Lou Harris & Associates recently identified 1,006 "peak performers" in U.S. companies and asked those star managers what kind of workplace they'd be most reluctant to leave. Fully 74 percent said, "One that promotes fun and closer work relationships with colleagues."

More and more successful companies have found that by intentionally incorporating fun at work they have increased teamwork, decreased employee absenteeism, reduced stress, enhanced customer service, and helped their employees achieve a sense of balance in their personal and professional lives.

What follows are five unusual ways to have more fun at work. These innovative techniques were invented by both management and nonmanagement employees and have been field-tested in a wide variety of industries. "Over and over again," reports *Fortune,* "people at the 100 Best Companies talk about how much fun they're having." It's time for your company to join them.

1. While it is not that unusual for an organization to name an Employee of the Month, Richland College in Dallas has turned the process of honoring its Employee of the Month into an unusual and fun-filled celebration. On the first Tuesday of each month, the president's staff—and all the willing participants they can gather along the parade route—wind their way through the campus in search of the employee who has been named for that month. (Any campus employee can be nominated for the honor by any individual or work group on campus.)

The parade moves through the campus with great fanfare, with marching music blaring from a boom box, streamers waving, and simple musical instruments accompanying, as the participants search for the honoree, whether she's teaching a class, working in the counseling center, having lunch in the cafeteria, or out riding a lawn mower. When the honoree is located, college president Stephen Mittelstet reads the Employee of the Month proclamation and presents assorted mementos in recognition of the event, including close-in parking privileges for the month, a plant grown by the horticulture department, and free movie tickets.

This simple little spirited exercise takes only about fifteen or twenty minutes each month; however, there is no question that it immensely boosts morale and esprit de corps on campus. Evelyn Wong, who is on the college's professional-support staff, is a past recipient of the award. She told me that she found the presentation to be one of the most "fun, exciting, and touching" experiences that she has had on the job. She said that it not only inspired her to be a better worker, but it also motivated her to start looking for the good work of other employees, so that she could then nominate them for the award.

Other participants commented about how good they feel being a part of the parade, even though they themselves have never received the honor. David Canine, one of the campus administrators, said, "I cannot tell you what positive experiences these parades engender for everyone involved. It sounds crazy to some people when I try to tell them about it, but it is truly a joyous experience for all of us every time it happens."

2. Julia MacKenzie-Walsh, who is a trainer for Shell petrol stations in London, created a "swearing room" for her coworkers. "We all need an outlet somewhere to let out our frustrations," says Julia. "So we set aside this little room where people could go to swear in peace. It was a room where no one could overhear them—except for me, of course, since I was next door. But I told them that I would be awarding points for particularly impressive swearing. The grand prize winner was, 'Gods' bees, and scrunties alight!' No, I haven't got a clue what it means, either, but we all thought it was very funny, and we all immediately started using it ourselves!"

3. Andrea Welch, the editor in chief of *Successful Meetings* magazine, sent a memo to her entire staff of fifty announcing that one day the following week would be Polka-Dot Day. The memo asked everyone to wear polka dots to work on that day, which would be "a celebration of polka dots of all varieties." The only formal "event" for the day was a group photo session, in which, according to Andrea's report, the staff posed in their "polka-dot dresses, shirts, ties, socks, scarves, and headbands. And no," she adds, before the question can be asked, "there weren't any itsy-bitsy, teenie-weenie, yellow polka-dot bikinis!"

Staff members got to keep copies of the photo as souvenirs,

and Andrea even published it in the magazine. "The whole day was fun and brought a well-deserved break in very busy schedules," she says. "It cost nothing. (Well, not quite. One editor did buy a spectacular black-and-white polka-dot shirt on the street for five dollars.) And the rewards in terms of morale were tremendous."

4. Dawn Morelli is a production engineering supervisor at Honeywell Satellite Systems in Phoenix. Dawn's colleagues nicknamed her the PEP Queen, because she had four Performance Enhancement Plans for her employees in operation at the same time. Dawn called one of these Performance Enhancement Plans "Where has all the time gone?"

In her office, Dawn hung up two calendars to mark the passage of time. The first one was a traditional calendar, but the second one was a giant wall calendar. On this calendar, Dawn marked off the days her team was able to save the organization by streamlining the production process. Dawn's team would examine a typical production process (like soldering, tinning, and bonding), and when they found ways to eliminate the waste, they added up the cycle time reduction on the giant calendar.

When she launched the program in August, Dawn threw a New Year's Day party for the office, replete with horns, party hats, and a Happy New Year cake. "When I ordered a Happy New Year cake in August, the lady at the bakery thought I was a total weirdo," Dawn recalls. "I brought in plastic champagne glasses, filled them with ginger ale, and we all did a toast to cycle time reduction. The people I work with thought the heat had gotten to me, and since it was August in Phoenix, that seemed like a likely explanation! But sometimes it's great to see your boss be a little goofy, because it helps everyone else loosen up and laugh. Our New Year's celebration helped my team unwind, then go back to work renewed, with even more energy for the project."

Any time her team was able to redesign a process to be more efficient, Dawn marked off the days the company had saved on her wall calendar. As the days flew by on her big wall calendar, whenever they reached a holiday, Dawn made sure they stopped to celebrate it.

"I gave out personalized holiday cards to everyone on our team when we reached Valentine's Day that same August. I prepared all the cards in advance, so we'd be ready as soon as we hit the holiday, because I'm a great believer in timely recognition. I also gave out bunches of chocolate kisses to everyone. Some of the team members didn't even eat the kisses. They just put them on display at their workstations as souvenirs, because they were so proud of our accomplishment."

When the team got to Easter—in September—Dawn gave out jelly beans to celebrate. On the "first day of spring," Dawn threw a picnic lunch for her team and presented each of them with a package of vintage baseball cards. On the "first day of summer," she was ready with a pizza party and some Honeywell monogrammed sunglasses.

After five months of the program, Dawn's staff had already celebrated two years' worth of holidays. And her department had helped increase Honeywell's on-time delivery rate to 87 percent, up from 75 percent the previous year.

5. Are you having enough fun at work? Take this quiz with your coworkers and find out!

1. You take "active fun breaks" on the job every day. +2
2. You take so many "active fun breaks" every day you figure you can give up your health-club membership and save five hundred bucks. +4
3. Your boss has a bad-hair day and takes it out on everyone. −3

4. Your boss encourages all employees to celebrate National Bad Hair Day by wearing wigs, bandannas, and crazy hats to the office. **+3**

5. Your manager orders surprise pizzas delivered to the loading dock. **+2**

6. Your boss accuses you of goofing off when you try to organize a paper-airplane-flying contest. **–5**

7. You have windup toys on your desk. **+2**

8. You are a card-carrying member of the "Are We Having Fun Yet?" Committee. **+3**

9. You change outfits in the middle of the day just to see if anyone notices. **+2**

10. You endorse your paycheck with a pen that looks like a rubber chicken. **+4**

How to interpret your score: Add total points scored in items 1–10.

0–5: Severely laughter-impaired.

6–10: Mildly fun-deprived.

11–19: You deserve a raise and some extra money.

—— 14—

Do
Something
Different

Anthropologist Ashley Montagu once told me that his goal in life was "to die young . . . at a ripe old age!" By this he meant that even as we inevitably grow older, we can still retain the life-affirming characteristics of our youth. No matter what problems and challenges we face, our daily lives can be filled with vitality, joy, playfulness, and a passion for new experiences. It doesn't matter how old you are—once you learn to laugh and play with life, you can feel young at heart, both at work and at home.

The key to dying young at a ripe old age is to constantly change the way you do things. Whenever you can, you break up your everyday routines, you change your ingrained work habits—in short, you do something different.

When Bill Campagna worked for Putnam Mutual Insurance, he recalls that "we had to constantly make split-second decisions, and we were always under extreme time pressure. So once a month I used to do this thing where I put up a sign on my cubicle that said, GERMAN ONLY SPOKEN HERE. Sometimes it was Italian, French, or Russian—anything but English. And when anyone dashed into my office to ask me an urgent question, I would refuse to answer unless they would speak to me in the accent of the day. If they tried to talk to me in a normal voice, I would just point to the sign and say, 'I am zo zorree, I cannot underztand a vord you are zaying.'

"They knew that if they wanted to get anything out of me, they had to talk in a fake accent, and as soon as they tried it, we would both crack up, laughing out of control. It worked every time. Because we were always building up so much tension at work, it was great to just bust it loose every once in a while. And making everybody talk in these fake accents, against their will, was the greatest stress-buster I ever dreamed up."

At the Ben & Jerry's scoop shop in Alexandria, Virginia, the scoopers have developed a number of original techniques to keep their jobs from becoming monotonous. These techniques also involve changing the way they speak to one another, to break up their normal routines. "It gets tiring scooping ice cream all day," remarks scooper Ellie Gompert. So the scoopers decided that for one day they could only refer to one another by their middle names.

"First of all, we had to learn everybody's middle names," Ellie remembers, "and that was fun, getting to know something new about the people I worked with every day. And as soon as we tried calling each other by our middle names, it created a lot of laughs. Because at first, whenever somebody called me by my middle name, if I was concentrating on something else, I wouldn't respond to it at all. They couldn't get my attention, because I wasn't used to hearing myself referred to that way. So then they'd have to get right in my face and say my middle name real loud and real slow, like I didn't even know my own name, and as soon as I caught on, then we'd both start laughing. And so it created a lot of energy among all the scoopers.

"On a Friday or Saturday night, when things are really busy, sometimes we'll have a rule that everyone has to speak in rhyme, like, 'I'm all out of cookie dough, and don't be tellin' me there ain't no mo'!' What's so funny for us is that everyone starts listening in on each other's conversations, because it's so much fun to eavesdrop on all these rhymes.

"We get a lot of tourists in our location, and they're all pretty burned out by the time they come in for ice cream. So we like to do unusual things to wake them up. Like when someone comes to the front of the line, we'll ask them something dopey like, 'Do you like ice cream?' Or 'Oooh, do you want some ice cream today?' The tourists always come alive when we joke around with them like that.

"We get to choose our own music to play in the store, and that always energizes us, too. In fact, there is a certain song on the *Grease* sound track, and whenever it comes on the stereo, we all stop whatever we're doing. All the scoopers break into this elaborately choreographed dance routine, behind the counter. It gives us a fun break whenever it happens, and the customers always love it."

The Brookline Booksmith normally closes at 11:00 P.M., but one time they decided to stay open all night. The bookstore announced in advance to their customers that they would be hosting a pajama party, and that night all the employees and most of their customers showed up in their pajamas. A live band played in the back of the store, refreshments were served, and there were games and contests, with store gift certificates as prizes. Employees handed out free souvenir nightcaps with the name of the bookstore printed on them to all the attendees. The unusual celebration was long remembered by customers and employees alike. "Just the other day," recalls store manager Dana Brigham, "I had a customer come up to me and tell me that she had just bought the perfect pair of pajamas, and so she wanted to know when were we going to do it again!"

When we walk in the office door feeling good from our life at home, we have a much greater chance of having a more playful and productive workday. For most people, life away from the job has a deep impact on emotional life at work. So it makes sense that we cannot establish an ongoing sense of joy and play in the workplace if we do not first establish it in our emotional life at home.

You might imagine that people whose jobs are not much fun would report a happy home life that more than counterbalances the enforced drudgery of their work lives. That has not been my experience, however. Over and over again, working people tell me that they not only don't have enough fun on the job, they don't know how to bring more joy, passion, and excitement into their lives away from the job, either. They want to have a more carefree and playful lifestyle at home, but they don't seem to be able to do it. People from all walks of life tell me that their life at home is not giving them all they need and want. Their message is always the same: "I know I need to lighten up my life, but I just don't know how."

I don't mean to imply that these people do not have a sense of meaning in their lives. Many are what we would usually call "successful" human beings in our society. Many are deeply religious. Many are fervently committed to wonderful projects and causes, gratifying relationships, and meaningful careers. Yet they still feel they are not taking the full measure of joy and happiness that life has to offer. They say that they are ready and willing to take the first step toward doing something different but they just don't know what to do.

And I say to them, "Sure you do. You've just told me what you need to do—you need to do something different! The first step in learning to live a life of play is to break out of your normal routines and to give yourself another perspective on your everyday life. Whatever you've been doing in your family relationships, for example, now is the time to do something different."

There are many families who dearly love one another but whose interactions have become dull and tiresome because their life together has become routine. The truth is that each one of us has the power to break that routine. But somebody has to take the first step.

Some years ago I was at my mother's house for our annual family gathering, and we were all dressed up in our holiday best. As always on these occasions, the time came for the yearly holiday photograph of the whole family. So we dragged ourselves out in the front yard and began the difficult process of getting fifteen people all lined up properly. "Okay, you change with Judith, you're taller. No, you kids get down in front. Al, why don't you hold the baby. Okay, Randy, *move in closer*!"

I felt a sense of déjà vu. I had done this same scene not once before, but at least 853 times. Not only that, I couldn't even remember seeing a single one of those pictures. We took the obligatory photo, then filed it away into oblivion. Our family photo had become a tradition that nobody really cared about but that everybody was resigned to suffering through together. We were all together as a family, but something important was missing—the fun of doing something different.

I trudged lifelessly over toward my assigned spot in the photo, and then all of a sudden I stopped dead in my tracks. I looked around at all these people I loved, all walking around like zombies. A mad impulse came over me, and I shouted out, "All right, hold it! Everybody, stop! Let's take this picture up on the roof!"

For just a moment, everyone looked at me with puzzled stares. Then smiles appeared on every face. All my relatives instantly sprang into action. What had been a dull routine suddenly became a family project. My cousins dashed to the garage to get ladders, my uncles planned out a strategy, and my aunts began tossing aside their high-heeled shoes. I expected some words of protest from my elderly grandmother, but no, she climbed right up the side of the house and sat on the roof with everyone else. Everyone picked out his or her own favorite spot—one straddled the gable, a couple balanced precariously on the ladder, and we all took a look around and grinned wildly.

Never underestimate the power of spontaneity, of doing something different from what you usually do. Sometimes that is all it takes to unleash the playful nature that lies dormant inside the most unlikely events—even your own family reunions. I don't have to tell you that when we go through the old family photo album it is the photo on the roof that everyone asks to see over and over again. It never fails to bring a smile to our faces, and we all come alive when we reminisce about that day. It didn't require anything special on our part other than allowing ourselves to be spontaneous, letting ourselves take delight in our own human spirit. We were all ready to come out and play.

15

Integrate Your Home Life and Work Life

Barbara Beck is Sprint's vice president of engineering and technical support for the western United States. Her passion is to help her employees achieve a sense of balance between their work lives and their home lives.

"The people getting all the awards at work are usually the people who need balance the most in their lives," says Barbara, "because they are dedicating so much of their time to work that they don't have the time left over to give to their families." So Barbara tries to give awards that will support the recipients in spending more time with their families—like a one-hundred-dollar gift certificate to a favorite restaurant, so an employee can take his or her spouse out to dinner. One employee who has seven children received passes for his whole family to go to Disneyland.

"When most managers write a memo of praise about an employee, they'll automatically send a copy to their boss, for their file," remarks Barbara, "but at Sprint we go a step further—we also send a copy to the employee's home, so it can be shared with the family." When two employees spent an entire weekend at work completing an emergency project, Barbara sent dried-flower wreaths to their wives; the accompanying note said, "I really appreciate you sharing your spouse with the company . . . and I want you to know that Sprint appreciates it, too."

"We know that an employee's home life directly impacts her attitude and performance on the job, so we try to integrate a person's family life into their work environment as much as we can," says Barbara. "Not only do we send family birthday cards to the homes of our employees, we take time out at work to publicly celebrate our children's accomplishments and awards at school." Barbara reports to Patti Manuel, who is the president of Sprint's business division. To bring a sense of family into work, Patti has set aside the wall next to her office as an art gallery for drawings and paintings done by her employees' children. One year Anne Morris, who also reports to Patti, thought of another way to link the office to home. She urged her coworkers to decorate their cubicles for Halloween, and on the big day all the Sprint employees brought their kids in to trick-or-treat from cubicle to cubicle.

Other holidays are celebrated at work as well. As you might imagine, Bring Your Daughter to Work Day gets a huge response from Barbara's coworkers. During the Easter holidays Barbara's entire office took twenty minutes off during the workday for an Easter egg hunt. "There were plastic Easter eggs hidden all over the office," recounts Barbara. "Some were filled with candy, and some had dollar bills stuffed inside. You would not believe how excited some of our people were to find a dollar bill for themselves hidden inside an Easter egg. Mind you, these are people making more than a hundred thousand dollars a year!"

Of course this concern with integrating home life and work life is not unique to Barbara Beck or to Sprint. Maria Fernanda dos Santos Teixeira, vice president of technical services for EDS in Brazil, chooses two employees each month who have been working overtime to help the company meet its commitments. "I send a note home to their families, telling them how much I appreciate the extra work this employee has been contributing to the company, and I send a huge bouquet of flowers along with the note. And I also send a check for five hundred dollars to the employee's spouse, with strict instructions to throw a big party at home celebrating his or her accomplishments at work."

Kris McMurray, general manager of radio station KLDE in Houston, knows that there are many days when her employees go home exhausted from work. So she has designated the first Friday of every month Stress-Release Friday, a day where the goal is for the employees to leave work more energized than when they arrived.

That day Kris hosts a free luncheon for her forty station employees. She presents "Mission Accomplished" awards, which are designed to recognize special achievements in sales and promotions and to welcome new employees; the entire staff decides on the winners. For the rest of the day Kris hires a masseuse to walk through the station giving neck and shoulder massages on request. Out in the parking lot all the employees' cars get a wash; and a bootblack roams the station giving out free shoeshines.

"Does it work?" I asked Kris.

"Does it ever!" she responded. "We have people coming to work on Stress-Release Friday with bags full of shoes to be shined. They bring in all their family's shoes, and all their neighbors' shoes, too! I tell them that my new motto is Clean feet make for happy employees. Like a lot of businesses, we used to be caught short-staffed on Fridays, with people calling in sick so they could have a long weekend. That never happens anymore. Why would you want to cut out for the weekend when it's so much more fun to come to work?"

Barbara Beck creates events for her staff at work that replicate the kind of celebrations they might have with their own families. "If you hold your regular staff meetings in different environments, you encourage new perspectives," Barbara believes. So she has conducted her staff meeting on the ferryboat to Catalina island. She has taken her staff for a picnic on the grass outside the office for a quick energy boost. Another time she took her direct reports out to a comedy club, right after their meeting had ended.

The behavior that Barbara models has inspired the attendees in her meetings to think similarly about their own meetings. One woman surprised her staff by holding a meeting at Universal Studios; since she was a director-level employee, she got herself a director's chair and Hollywood-style sunglasses for all the other employees to wear during the day. When the formal meeting was ended, they all went on the amusement-park rides. "And of course we commemorate all these adventures with eight-by-ten framed photos," says Barbara. "It's been three years since some of these events, and I still see the photos on people's desks, so obviously it's still meaningful to them after all this time."

Barbara once tried a variation of the company shopping spree: she gave each of her staff a hundred dollars to spend on themselves in an hour, with the caveat that the winner would be the person who came the closest to spending exactly one hundred dollars. The winner was a man who bought fifteen different items and brought back receipts totaling ninety-nine dollars and change. The most stunning entrant was a woman who bought herself a four-hundred-dollar Gucci purse; "Hey, the extra hundred bucks really helped put me over the top!" she joked.

"An added benefit to all the fun," claims Barbara, "is that when you go off-site, you make contact with people you ordinarily wouldn't interact with, and that gives you the opportunity to develop new customers. It's obvious that our people perform better when they're enjoying themselves. I try to point out to my managers that if their employees are happy, then they stay with the company longer, and we save the huge training costs of replacing personnel that we could have kept on board if they felt appreciated and valued."

A heavy workload can leave Sprint employees little time for volunteer work in the community. So Barbara mandates that each of her line managers must get off the premises with his or her team at least once a year and get involved with a charity or a community-service project. Her teams have worked with Habitat for Humanity, AIDS Walk, Project Open Hand, and the local school systems. "It's possible to stay within the HR guidelines and still have your people do something like volunteer four hours a month in the local schools, whether they are parents or not," she says. "And in every case, doing the volunteer work together away from the job has supported our team-building efforts back at work. And it's given the parents in our organization a better chance to participate in the lives of their kids."

16

Find a Child to Be Your Teacher

Ted McCarthy had a job selling commercial flooring for industrial use, and he was working on one of the largest deals of his career. The project was worth well over a million dollars and was one of the most lucrative sales in the history of his company.

Because of the size of this sale, the president of Ted's company wanted to meet the client. And the president of the client company wanted to meet with Ted as well. As Ted prepared to leave that day for the office, his two-year-old son walked up to him and said, "Daddy, do good today. I help." Ted kissed his son and headed off to work.

"I felt proud as the president of my company and I drove to the client's location," Ted remembers. "I knew the deal was done, and all I had to do was complete this final meeting. My contact at the client site was as excited to finish this as I was. He would head this project for his company, and it would be a real feather in his cap, since this would be the largest expansion they had ever had. I was determined that I would do everything in my power to make my contact look good within his company. He trusted me, and I would repay that trust with the best job my company had ever provided.

"When we were shown into the conference room, I could hardly contain my excitement. My contact and his president entered the room a few minutes later. Everyone shook hands, and we all sat down. I began the meeting by outlining the plan my contact and I had developed over the last few months. It's difficult to say at what point I lost control of the meeting, but after a few minutes, it became evident that my president and the client's president could not stand each other."

Ted watched in horror as the project he had invested months of work on began to crumble before his eyes. Ted's contact just stared at him, shell-shocked, as the two company presidents hurled barbed insults at each other. "I looked at the clock on the wall, and what seemed like hours in this room had been only minutes," Ted recalls.

"My thoughts raced through my mind for any possible way to save this deal. The second hand on the clock seemed to move in slow motion, tick-tock, tick-tock. A possibility leaped into my mind. In my briefcase I had the engineer's study that was the basis of our entire proposal. Perhaps I could use it to get the two presidents to refocus on business."

Ted opened his briefcase, and he suddenly realized what his young son had meant that morning when he had said, "Daddy, I help." Unbeknownst to Ted, his son had evidently removed all of his father's files and left in its place his own favorite toy, a red plastic hammer. The hammer had a squeaker in each end, "so when you hit it against something, it went squeak-squeak-squeak. At this point the stress was too much for me. I completely forgot where I was, or what I was doing. Without thought, I picked up the hammer and hit it repeatedly against my head. The room filled with the piercing noise, as the hammer went squeak-squeak-squeak against my head.

"What brought me back into the room was a sound even louder than the hammer—laughter. As my eyes refocused on the room around me, I saw that everyone was laughing. Realizing what I had just done, I joined in the laughter. It seemed to go on for minutes, I don't remember. I just know tears were coming out of my eyes, and my sides hurt. And the tension had completely disappeared from the room. Wiping the tears from his eyes, my client's president signed the contract for us to begin the work to install their flooring. My president shook his hand and told him that this was the best meeting he had ever attended. My contact praised me for all the excellent work I had done. My emotions felt like a piano that had just had the most difficult symphony played upon it.

"I learned a few lessons that day," Ted concluded. "The truth was, ninety percent of my success was due to love. My love of work, my love of doing a good job, my love for the clients who trust and believe in me, and my love for my family. And especially, I thought of my son, and how much he had helped me that day. For years afterward, I would tell him that he had made his first sale that day."

One of the best ways to learn about a new subject is to study with a teacher who is an expert in that subject. Fortunately, there are thousands of perfect teachers out there in the world who can help us learn to laugh and play with life. They are those individuals who are noted for their love of play—children.

"Wait just a minute," I can hear some of you saying. "You should meet some of the children I know. Those little crumb-snatching, curtain-climbing, narcissistic brats don't strike me as such great teachers. And if my kid started stealing files out of my briefcase, believe me, I don't think the story would have a happy ending!"

You're right, and I'm not suggesting that we should act like children. Obviously, our childhood is a developmental stage we need to grow through and beyond. Although there is nothing wrong with that developmental stage, I think it would be a bad idea to get stuck there forever. The important distinction to make here is between childish behaviors and childlike attitudes. It is possible to be childlike in our approach to playing with life, without at the same time being childish in the way we interact with other people. That is why that same best-selling book that tells us to "turn and become as children" also tells us to "put away childish ways."

All of us still carry within us the child we once were. If we could merely rediscover and embrace the virtues of that child, then laughing and playing with life would come much more easily. A good way to start that rediscovery process is to find some child with whom you can play. I highly recommend that your teacher be under the age of six. It's been my experience that children under six years of age are usually characterized by playful, creative, spontaneous behavior. Older children may have shifted into the more logical, analytical way of being that is typical of adult behavior. Our educational system generally rewards conformity, not creativity, logical and systematic thinking, not spontaneity and playfulness. The more time we spend in the educational system the more we are rewarded for finding the one "correct" answer. Intuitive thinking goes largely unrewarded, and by the time you get to college you have entered a virtual temple of worship to logical thinking. So your best teacher will likely not have seen the inside of a schoolhouse.

After you locate a child to be your teacher, then you will need to get down on the floor and play together, or perhaps the two of you can take a trip to a park. Do not, I repeat, do not forget who is the teacher and who is the student. Your goal is to relearn from the child the art of play. Try to forget all of your adult desires to control the interaction, lay out the rules, make it competitive, find a way to determine a winner—you will only ruin it for the child as play, and for yourself as a learning experience.

Your only role is to be a student. You are there as a participant observer to learn how to laugh and play with life, to develop a new attitude. You are there to rediscover the childlike virtues that you need before you can become a more playful adult.

Children see each new situation with fresh eyes. They teach us how much we adults could enrich our lives if we would actually *see* the world, not just look at it, not just let it pass before our eyes. In order to laugh and play with life we need to really look at it, to let life "speak" to us, and then see it as it is. While playing with my young daughter, I have often been reminded that I need to continually open my ears, eyes, and heart to other human beings.

One day when my daughter, Rachel, was nearly six years old we were driving through an older section of town. While we were stopped at an intersection for a traffic light, I looked across the street and saw a person dressed in ragged, tattered clothes. He looked to me as though he hadn't had more than a few hours' sleep in the last week, and he had a wine bottle hanging out of his pocket. He was standing on the corner, waiting to cross the street in our direction. My daughter and I were both sort of staring at him, although we were pretending not to.

I felt as though I needed to say something to Rachel about this man. I probably saw it as an opportunity for a teachable moment, in which I would impart to my young daughter some little lesson in life. The man was gazing up at the sky and appeared to be mumbling to himself. I looked at Rachel a little uncomfortably, because I was unsure of what I should say, only sure that I must say something. I finally said, "Rachel, what do you suppose that guy's doing?"

She looked back at me with an open and thoughtful face and said, "I don't know, Dad. Maybe he's writing a poem." Another teachable moment that wasn't wasted! Another time of confusion about who was the teacher and who was the student! I had looked at the man and failed to see "person," I had seen "bum." I was closed off to seeing him in any way but in my own preconceived categories. I saw him in a narrow, limited way, as an object of my own creation. My daughter had seen this man as a person, as a possibility. Her possibilities even included those persons whom I admire greatly, the poets. Unlike her father, she didn't already "know" who he was just by looking.

I know this sounds like a rather simple little story that merely serves to let a proud father go on about his darling child. And although that may be true, I think this story can give us an insight into the kind of attitude we adults need to develop so we can instantly create potential playmates for ourselves every day, with almost every person we encounter.

Why is it so much harder to make new friends the older we get? Why is it that the world seems filled with so many playmates when we are children, and with so many jerks when we are grown up? It is because as children we allow ourselves a willingness and an optimism about potential relationships, while as adults we are full of instant judgments and doubts about the people we meet.

If we already "know" what's going to happen in a particular situation with a particular person, then we can almost be sure to experience it in just that way. We are cautious in our interactions, and we subconsciously look for evidence that will prove our initial judgments to be correct. But once we begin to spend some time in the company of children, we can learn to look, instead, with the eyes of a child once again. If we can look at both the people we love and the people we barely know as potential playmates, the way children look at one another, then I assure you that much of the time we will bring that playful part out of them, and they will truly become playmates for us. I don't think it is too radical a notion to suggest that those individuals who go through life looking to find the good in others and trying to bring out the joy in everyone they meet are the people most likely to find what they are looking for.

17

Learn to
Receive Recognition

Many organizations have developed their own unique, playful way of personally recognizing the accomplishments of their employees. At Pizza Hut, president Mike Rawlings presents award recipients with a personally autographed "Cheese Head" hat. At Kentucky Fried Chicken, president Jeff Moody presents a floppy rubber chicken as a coveted award. And at Taco Bell, president Peter Waller carries a ladle with a large plastic pepper attached to it and, by touching the award recipient on the shoulder with this "pepper scepter," inducts him or her into the Royal Order of the Pepper.

Of course in all of these successful companies, it is not just the president of the organization but all employees who are encouraged to recognize one another's accomplishments. Learning to give praise, to publicly recognize the accomplishments of your coworkers, is an important skill for all working people to develop. But although there are many courses of study that teach employees how to give effective, timely, positive feedback, there are almost no courses that I know of that teach employees a related, equally important skill—how to *receive* positive feedback.

Whenever speech coach Lee Glickstein sees one of his students attempt to leave the stage as soon as he has finished his speech but before the audience has finished applauding, he rushes the stage and pushes the student back into the spotlight. "Take your applause," Lee whispers into the student's ear. "Remember to take your applause!"

Not all of us can have the experience of a roomful of people enthusiastically applauding our efforts. But all of us get the chance to receive positive feedback from other people every day, in the form of compliments. A compliment is applause on an individual level, a form of specific, outside feedback telling us what things we are doing well.

Unfortunately, our typical business culture teaches us not to accept compliments but to deny or deflect them instead. This is called being modest.

Imagine this typical situation. You're walking down the street on your lunch hour, and you run into an old friend, who says to you admiringly, "Hey, you look great!" Your most immediate response would probably be:

1. Denial: "Oh, I do not! My hair is awful, and I just threw on the first thing I found in the closet this morning." or

2. Deflection: "So do you! You look just great! Really. No kidding. You look fantastic!"

Denial and deflection are lessons that we all learn at an early age. That's why if a colleague at work compliments you on a job well done, your first impulse is probably to minimize your accomplishments and say it was nothing. If instead you were to respond to a compliment from a team member by agreeing with

it, and by then affirming that you are indeed a brilliant, powerful, and lovable person, your coworker would probably look at
you like you had lost your mind. We have names for people who
talk about themselves like that, the kindest of which are "ego-
maniac," "self-centered," and "abnormal."

And so our culture rewards us for feeling bad about ourselves. Even worse, it rewards us for not telling the truth when
we feel good about ourselves.

We teach the employees who attend our Playfair seminars
that the ability to give positive feedback to one another is an
essential business skill, and we urge them, in Ken Blanchard's
wonderful phrase, to "catch somebody doing something right."
Then we ask for volunteers from the audience who are already
good at giving compliments to the important people in their
lives to come up onstage. We remind the rest of the audience
that nobody ever gets enough positive feedback, and that this
group of their colleagues deserves to get something back in return for all the positive feedback they've been giving out.

Then we ask all the seminar participants to visualize themselves at the most spectacular concert they've ever attended,
to imagine giving an enormous standing ovation to the performers, to triple that energy, and to give the people onstage
the most spectacular standing ovation they've ever dreamed of.

Needless to say, the entire place goes wild—people yelling,
screaming, standing on chairs, lighting matches and waving
them around their heads. And not only is it wonderful to watch
the faces of the people onstage come alive with joy and excitement as they receive this ovation, it's equally moving to watch
the faces of the audience members fill with joy as they are delivering the applause. After the volunteers return to their seats,
the rule is that anyone in the audience who wants to can ask for
a standing ovation at any time during the rest of the program.

At a meeting of Sprint employees in Nashville, the entire

group went out to the Grand Ole Opry, the country-music mecca, the evening after the Playfair session. Between acts, during a long break in the entertainment, one of the Sprint employees got inspired to stand up on his chair and yell out, "I want a standing ovation!" His colleagues reported that he received a bigger standing ovation from the audience that night than any of the performers.

In just the way that having a whole roomful of people give you a standing ovation can make you feel great, so, too, your spirits can be lifted when you listen to a compliment without deflecting it, discounting it, or denying it. These little everyday moments of applause can be just as nourishing to your well-being as the big, once-in-a-lifetime ones.

The next time you receive a compliment, notice your initial reaction. Do you try to deny or deflect it? Do you feel embarrassed by hearing yourself praised? If this is your usual way of responding to compliments, try instead to say to the person giving you the compliment: "Thank you, you are incredibly perceptive!" Probably, after the initial moment of shock, you will both break out laughing. And think of what you've done. You've accepted the compliment, you've thanked the person for noticing, and you've given a compliment in return, all in one sentence. And as a bonus, you've shared a laugh together.

Once you've become comfortable responding to compliments this way, it's time to move on to the advanced version: "Thank you. The better you get to know me, the more you're going to like me!"

It's so much fun to tell the truth, isn't it?

Receiving positive feedback is just as important a skill to learn as giving it. The next time someone gives you a compliment, why not let it in? Remember to take your applause!

18

Celebrate International Fun at Work Day

If the upper management of your organization is resistant to the idea of fun at work, you can introduce them to a holiday celebrated at such companies as IBM, Pacific Bell, AT&T, EDS, Sprint, and even the Federal Reserve Bank: International Fun at Work Day.

If you look in Chase's Official Calendar of Events, you will see that April 1 (or the first Thursday in April, if April 1 falls on a weekend) has been officially designated as International Fun at Work Day. This coming April, why not organize your workplace in an International Fun at Work Day celebration? From coast to coast, hundreds of other organizations will be busy celebrating along with you. On previous Fun at Work Days, for example:

• More than three thousand Sprint employees in twenty different cities went on a "photo safari" armed with disposable cameras. Each team was charged with bringing back photos of themselves in unusual team-building situations from the photo-safari instruction list, e.g., waiting tables in a restaurant, sitting on a police car, perched in a tree, or playing catch with a dog.

• Employees of A Business Conference Call in Chaska, Minnesota, celebrated the day as Backward Day. They came to work dressed backward, talked backward ("Now lunch to going am I"), and finished the day's celebration with an upside-down cake.

• At the Grafton Public Library in Grafton, Ohio, the party lasted for twelve consecutive hours, with a different employee being celebrated every hour.

• The workers at the Kansas State University Bookstore all changed jobs for the afternoon.

• At Sun Microsystems employees built a workstation at the bottom of a shark tank.

Need more fun ideas? Here are some other unusual ways to celebrate the day with your coworkers:

• Ask all employees to bring in baby photos, pet pictures, or high school–yearbook photos to post on the bulletin board. Then guess who's who, or whose pet is whose.

• Hold a lottery where the winner gets driven to and from work in the company limo. (If you don't have a company limo, rent one for the day.)

• Offer your employees some unusual gifts, like free housecleaning certificates, to celebrate the day.

• Bring in a bouquet of flowers and present it to one of your coworkers with the instructions, "I want you to keep this on your desk for the next half hour. Then pass it on to someone else and tell them to do the same."

• Take some joy breaks during the day, where you teach all the employees the art of scarf juggling or play marbles together.

• Hire an on-site masseuse for the day.

• Take a group portrait of your office mates dressed up for Clash Dressing Day, Suspender Day, or Pajama Day.

• Dog Days of Spring: Let all employees bring their pets to work with them.

• Hide clown noses around the office and announce a clown-nose hunt.

• Have all employees switch jobs for an hour. One employee gets the opportunity to have the company president do his job for the day, while he trains and supervises.

Just as the staff at *Successful Meetings* magazine celebrated Christmas in July, you don't have to wait until April 1 to celebrate National Fun at Work Day. Anytime is the right time to celebrate. How about organizing a Fun at Work Day at your office next week?

Of course, it is possible that you may work in the most dull and fun-deprived work environment in the known world, with coworkers who are much better at mental torture than at having fun at work. Or maybe you work at home alone, or in a one-person office. These problems should not stop you from celebrating Fun at Work Day; after all, if absolutely necessary, we can always have fun all by ourselves. I've often made myself laugh out loud when I was all alone.

Even a silly, token gesture can start you off in the right direction. Buy yourself a windup toy for your desk to celebrate the day. Or buy several, and you'll have started a new collection. Let those little toy feet scurry across your desk every hour on the hour, and I guarantee it will put you in the frame of mind to celebrate Fun at Work Day. Notice how different the quality of your telephone conversations can become, how much more open to laughter and play you can be that day, once you remember that thousands of other people across the country are celebrating along with you.

Many things in life take at least two people—tennis, marriage, Monopoly, to name just a few. Luckily, having fun only takes one.

19

Take Your Message to City Hall

Once you've organized your office in celebrating Fun at Work Day, it's time to take to the streets and get the city government involved. Ask the mayor to issue a proclamation declaring Fun at Work Day in your local community. To give the mayor some inspiration, here are sample proclamations from Ronald Kirk, the mayor of Dallas, and San Francisco mayor Willie Brown.

Office of the Mayor/City of Dallas Proclamation

Whereas, according to U.S. government statistics, American worker productivity has recently had its best showing since 1992; and

Whereas, productivity gains are crucial to increases in corporate profits and individual living standards; and

Whereas, in the twenty-first century, it will be critical for employers to embrace the concept of creating change in the workplace; and

Whereas, there is a correlation between playfulness and productivity; and

Whereas, employees who enjoy coming to work are more productive, more loyal, and stay with companies longer; and

Whereas, fun at work is a proven way for any organization to reduce employee stress, improve morale, build a team, and, ultimately, increase the bottom line; and

Whereas, April 1 has been designated as National Fun at Work Day.

Now, therefore, I, Ronald Kirk, Mayor of the City of Dallas, and on behalf of the Dallas City Council, do hereby proclaim April 1 as Fun at Work Day in the City of Dallas.

City and County of San Francisco Proclamation

Whereas, on April 1 from coast to coast, organizations will be celebrating Fun at Work Day to increase productivity and smiles in the workplace; and

Whereas, there is a direct correlation between playfulness and productivity, and employees who enjoy work are more productive, more loyal, and stay with their companies longer; and

Whereas, engaging employees in fun at work is a proven way for any organization to reduce stress, improve morale, facilitate teamwork, and ultimately increase the bottom line; and

Whereas, of the thirteen lucky ways to celebrate Fun at Work Day, a Mayor's Office favorite is to bring in champagne (or sparkling apple juice) and take the time to

> *toast one another's successes and fabulous failures of the past few weeks;*
> *Now, therefore, be it resolved, that I, Willie L. Brown, Jr., Mayor of the City and County of San Francisco, honor the importance of having a little fun, and do hereby proclaim April 1 as Fun at Work Day in San Francisco.*

The battle cry of "Take your message to city hall" can be taken literally, or it can be viewed as a metaphor for advancing the cause of laughter and play with anyone in a position of power or influence—the CEO, your immediate supervisor, or some other work leader. Any one of us can appoint ourselves ambassador of playfulness to these people in positions of power.

We must always remember, however, that just because we take our message to city hall, it doesn't always mean that anyone will listen. History is filled with examples of prophets—including prophets of play—whose messages either were not heard or were summarily rejected. It is important to remember in such situations that change often takes time, and not to give up.

My wife and I once lived in a small town in Mexico, right by a dirt road that was used as the bypass for people traveling to and from the city of Taxco. Every day scores of trucks rumbled past our house, stirring up dust. It was as though we were living much of each day in a huge dust storm. My wife had noticed that not only was our health being affected by the dust but also that many neighborhood children were suffering horribly. So she decided to take action.

After several telephone calls to the mayor's office were not returned and she was unable to reach a solution with the mayor's secretary, she decided that it was time to take her message to city hall. We arrived at the mayor's office believing that our personal visit was bound to get some action. However, when we got there we discovered that the opposing political party was having a demonstration against the mayor, and they had actually occupied the entire city hall. Protestors held signs, and banners hung from city hall windows accusing the mayor of everything from broken promises to political assassination.

The look on my wife's face told me that she understood perfectly that the mayor had other things on his mind than her little dust-bowl drama; he was busy fighting for his political life.

However, she didn't give up. She was able to laugh about the whole political situation and then take steps in her own personal battle against the dust. She enlisted the neighbors' help in watering down the street on a regular basis, and she placed several large rocks in strategic locations in the road. The trucks had to slow down somewhat to navigate around the rocks, and so they kicked up far less dust.

The mayor may not have been ready to listen, but in the end my wife was able to address the problem in her own creative way. This is exactly the challenge that each of us has when we take our message to city hall. It's good to remember that even if our message of fun and play falls on deaf ears, that doesn't mean we shouldn't preach it loud and clear. At least you will have mobilized the most important person involved in the case—yourself.

Thank Your Boss for Firing You

Most of us are trained to look at the dark side of things, rather than the bright side. When you get a performance review and your supervisor points out nineteen areas where you are doing well and one area where you need to improve, what sticks in your mind? If you're like most people, you spend the rest of the day worrying about the one place where you got low ratings, obsessing about the negative instead of celebrating the positive.

And when something truly bad happens, then we really beat ourselves up. Let us suppose, for example, that your boss singles you out for criticism at a staff meeting and you feel publicly humiliated. You go home at night, and all you can do is replay the incident over and over in your mind. You can hardly pay attention to your family. You feel agitated and fearful. You lie awake at night, brooding. What can you do to lighten things up for yourself?

If life is a game for you, then the first thing to do is to ask yourself questions like "What was this last play all about? What is the hidden message here for me? Is it even possible that some good can actually come out of this miserable situation? Might it possibly be some kind of a blessing in disguise?"

Jim McGory worked in corporate sales for a major airline. At his annual review, Jim's manager told him that his numbers were terrific but that at this company that wasn't good enough. "He told me that when we went to intercompany meetings, I was always the first to take off my jacket," Jim recalls. "That was a sign to him that I wasn't professional enough. Then he told me that when he came by my desk he would hear me laughing on the telephone. 'That's not really acceptable,' he said to me.

"But the reason I'm laughing on the phone is because I'm having a good time with my customers!" Jim protested. "The reason my numbers are so good is because I treat my customers like my friends."

"Jim, you have to remember that in business, perception is reality," responded his boss. "If people hear you laughing, then they won't believe you're doing a good job."

Jim shook his head sadly, in disbelief, as he recounted this story. "That's when the lightbulb went on, and I realized it was time to get out and start my own businesss." So Jim founded MAP Promotions and Incentives, which provides travel promotions, sweepstakes, and incentive programs for corporate clients. "I wanted to create a place where people can laugh on the phone with their customers and it won't seem weird. In my business now we have four television sets in the office, and music playing all the time. I wanted to create a place where people could work hard but where they could have a good time, too. I wanted to make a work environment as friendly and homelike as possible."

Much of the time we cannot foresee the consequences of

our actions, and things that look disastrous in the short view can turn out to be a necessary part of a bigger picture. "When I think about my old boss," Jim recalls, "I remember that he didn't understand me at all. But the main thing I remember is that he forced me out the door and forced me to become a millionaire!"

How you react to a given situation with your boss can depend on your point of view about what is happening to you. I once saw this point poignantly illustrated at a workshop I attended. One of the participants said to the workshop leader, "I'm just a total failure in love. Every time I fall in love with someone, he walks out on me and breaks my heart."

The workshop leader asked her, "Now, exactly how many men are you talking about here?"

She laughed and said, "Three."

The leader said to her, "Okay, I want you to think about the first man for a moment. You really loved him, didn't you?"

"Yes," she replied thoughtfully.

"And now think about the second man. You loved him even more than the first one, didn't you?"

"Yes, I did."

"So can you take a moment and thank that first man for getting out of your life, and opening up the space for you to meet the second man?"

The young woman was obviously startled by this suggestion. She thought about it for a moment and grudgingly admitted, "Yeah, I guess I can."

"And now think about the last guy. You loved him the most of all, didn't you?"

She nodded, not sure where this was headed.

"And was it partly because you had loved the second man so well that you knew how to love the third man so well?"

"But he was more to me than just practice for somebody else!" she protested. "I really loved him!"

"Of course you did," the group leader pressed on. "You really loved him at the time. And he loved you too. And remembering that, and thinking very kindly of him all the time now, can you thank him for helping you to learn how to love deeply, and then for getting out of your life, so you could have the chance to meet the third man?"

She looked back at him thoughtfully. "Yes," she said softly. "I suppose so."

"Life is not static," the leader continued passionately. "Life is always changing. Can you see that in your experience of romance with these men you have not been standing still? Instead, it is as though you have been moving up a staircase. And with each step you have been able to love more deeply, and you have been able to attract a more powerful type of man to you each time. You're telling me that the climb is steep, and that you're tired. I know you are. You're telling me that you want to stop before you get to the top of the staircase. Do you really want to give up on yourself? Do you really want to settle for less of a life than you really deserve to have?

"Right now, can you thank that last guy for dumping you and getting out of your life and making way for the next incredible romance that is undoubtedly on its way for you very soon? Can you imagine what kind of a man must be waiting for you on the very top step?"

With a look of profound recognition on her face, the woman just sat down without saying another word.

All of us want life to be easy and simple. All of us resist change. For example, many times we will put up with an uncomfortable situation at work, just so we don't have to go through the greater discomfort of looking for a new job. We pretend to ourselves that things aren't as bad as they look, we hide the truth from ourselves, until finally things get so bad that we are forced into action.

When your boss humiliates you in front of your colleagues, you might finally be forced to admit to yourself that something is dreadfully wrong. You might finally ask yourself how you can continue to put up with a supervisor who doesn't appreciate you; you may wonder why you haven't left this job long ago. Like the woman at the workshop who was worried about being rejected by her lovers without appreciating her own growth and power, you too may have been clinging to one small step, when in fact the whole staircase has opened up ahead of you.

Is it time to transfer out to another department? Have you learned enough during your time on this job that you are qualified to move on to a better job? Is it possible that you will soon be looking back at this situation from a far distance, wondering why you didn't make the change sooner? Like Jim McGory, you may find that a whole new world awaits you.

Now, can you thank your boss for inadvertently giving you the impetus to change your life for the better?

21

Don't
Be Afraid
to Be a Fool

If you want to bring more laughter and play into your life, it is sometimes necessary, as my grandmother found out on the roof, to do things that you might ordinarily think of as foolish. The archetype of the fool plays an important role in human history and has something important to teach us all; that is why some of the greatest spiritual teachers were fools. It is the fool who challenges us to take risks, to leave our zone of safety and try new things. The fool invites us to turn things upside down and investigate new possibilities. The fool is spontaneous, laughs at conventional behavior, and, by example, constantly urges us on to explore life more fully.

I sometimes hear people say that they are afraid of being made to look like a fool. Of course, no one wants to appear foolish, but that's because we misunderstand the legacy of the fool. The fool has actually been a powerful, positive image throughout human history. We can find the fool prominently portrayed in Shakespeare, Erasmus, and Aristophanes. Virtually every religion includes the idea and image of the fool, whose job is to help us to avoid taking ourselves too seriously. As an old saying has it, "The wise have more to learn from the fool than a fool from the wise."

When Playfair's Fran Solomon gave a presentation to Choice Hotels International about the importance of having fun at work, she told a story about a hotel executive who purchased a pair of Tweety Bird slippers from the hotel gift shop for himself, then caused a minor sensation among his employees as he toured the hotel property in his new slippers, with a final stop at the shoeshine stand and the Tiki Bar.

John Ruzik, owner of the Quality Suites Resort in Tampa, Florida, was in the audience for Fran's talk. When he returned home he told his employees that it was important to have more fun at work, and he told them about the Tweety Bird slippers. Several days later, one of the front-desk employees made a major accounting mistake that had John seeing red. To prevent himself from totally losing it, John stormed out of the front office and into the kitchen, where he ran into one of his assistant managers who was wearing a pair of Scooby Doo slippers. "At that moment I truly realized the benefits of having fun at work," recounts John. "I started laughing so hard at the sight of this guy in his goofy slippers that I was practically crying. And of course all of the tension about the accounting mistake went right out the window."

John immediately went out shopping for cartoon-animal slippers for all his managers. He returned to the hotel with Daffy Duck slippers, Bugs Bunny slippers, and Muppet slippers. Every day the Quality Suites has a manager's reception, where the hotel guests can enjoy free drinks, and meet one another and the hotel staff. As he distributed the animal slippers,

John announced that each of his managers was required to attend the manager's reception for a minimum of twenty minutes each day—wearing their animal slippers. "I can tell that the hotel guests love to see the managers in their slippers," says John, "and it's a great conversation starter. One time one of our assistant managers was working late on a project, and he dashed over to the manager's reception in his regular shoes. So one of the guests came over to him and said, 'Hey, aren't you a manager? Where are your slippers?'

"Wearing their slippers every day has created a great sense of spirit among the managers," John concludes. "I have no doubt that this kind of foolishness has turned out to be very productive for us." The following month Fran Solomon was invited to give a follow-up talk at Choice Hotels. John ran up to the stage at the end of her program and presented Fran with a plaque featuring a photo of all of his managers gathered together in their slippers. And in appreciation of the difference she had made to the morale at the Quality Suites, John presented Fran with a pair of Tweety Bird slippers to call her own.

In Eastern thought there is something called the "law of reversed effect." This law suggests that a thing is generated out of its opposite—you will not find a thing in nature without also finding its opposite. There will be no inside without an outside. No mountain will be found without a valley. No wave exists without a trough. No up is available without a down.

I've noticed that most of us like to think of ourselves as sane, sensible people. But if the law of reversed effect is true, then there must also be a fool within each of us, just waiting to be liberated. If we really want to fill our lives with laughter and play, then it is not enough to find a fool or two to hang around with sometimes. Instead, we must be willing—at least at times—to find our own inner fool and let that fool come out and play. We must allow ourselves to do the unexpected, to take a risk, to turn things upside down. We must give ourselves permission to wear Tweety Bird slippers whenever the fancy strikes us. Not only will our lives then be more blessed with joy, but we will also bring more joy to those around us. Of course, once you invite your fool to emerge, it is likely that he or she will choose to appear at the most unlikely times, and in the most embarrassing situations.

This certainly was true for me the time I "customized" my car. During the days when I was famous among my friends for refusing to drive anything but inexpensive used cars, I was also at the height of my powers as a long-distance runner. As we were walking by my garage one day, my friend Peter Alsop noticed two cardboard boxes that I had stored on the floor in the back of the garage. He could see the glimmer of silver and gold reflected in the light bouncing back from the cartons. He paused to get a better look. "What have you got in there?" he asked me.

"Oh, just my old running trophies," I explained.

"Really?" he asked me, intrigued. "What are you going to do with them?"

"What am I going to do with them?" I laughed. "Nothing. I'm going to keep them in boxes. I've had these boxes for years. Every time I get a new trophy I just throw it in one of the boxes."

"You're kidding!" said Peter, moving in to get a closer look. "You're really not going to do anything with all these trophies?"

"What am I supposed to do with them?" I asked him. "Can you imagine me having a trophy room in my house? Can you imagine what my friends would say?" We both laughed at the idea.

"I have a fun idea," said Peter, holding a few of the statuettes up to the light as he examined them more closely. "Can I have them?"

I paused for a long moment to consider his request. I began to worry slightly. I had known Peter long enough to know that deep within his artistic soul a trickster was alive and well. He had that unnerving gleam in his eye that usually meant he was about to involve me in some kind of crazy project. "Sure, I guess you can have them," I told him hesitantly. "What are you going to do with them?"

"First let me see what we've got," he said, grinning. So we emptied out the boxes and started to inventory our cache. There were piles of medals and plaques, but Peter wasn't interested in them. All he wanted to see was the trophies. There were forty-nine in all. Some were silver-painted, some were golden. Some were five inches tall, but most were double that size. All of them had runners mounted on a trophy base in the identical position, left arm angled out ahead, left foot kicking up behind.

Forty-six of the runners were men, and three were women. How I got the women's trophies I'm not sure. Sometimes at the end of a race there's a lot of confusion when it's time for the trophies to be handed out. There have been many times when I've had to leave before the awards ceremony and one of my friends would say, "Don't worry. I'll stick around and pick up your trophy for you." And they'd grab whatever trophy they could find. Man, woman, they knew I wouldn't care. After all, a trophy is a trophy.

Peter unscrewed one of the statuettes from its base and held it up triumphantly in front of him. He looked me straight in the eye. "What would you think," he asked me, trying to keep a straight face but not succeeding very well, "if we mounted all of these runners on the top of your car!"

I hoped he was joking, but I could tell right away that he wasn't. Stunned, I thought about his proposal for a few moments. After all, my car was just a beat-up old station wagon, but she was also my only set of wheels. I even had an affectionate nick-name for her: Jewel. I mean, this was a really funny idea, but after all, Peter would be flying back home to Los Angeles in a few days, and I would be left behind living with the car. On the other hand, if I said no way, then my reputation as a player would be severely questioned.

I grinned back at him. "Sure," I said. "Let's do it!"

We borrowed a drill and bought some nuts and rubber wash-ers. "Don't worry," Peter assured me, "these washers will pro-tect you in case it rains on the car after we've drilled all the holes in the roof. I hope."

We removed the inside roof of the car and started drilling. We drilled forty holes in all, with the runners bunched together in a pack at the back of the roof, then spaced out across the rest of the roof as the pack thinned out the way it would in any race. Then we glued two of the runners racing down the windshield, finishing up with nine runners mounted across the hood in a mad dash for the finish line. We put the three women runners in the number-one, number-seven, and number-thirty posi-tions, wondering if anyone but us would ever notice that a woman was in the lead.

Then we took the car out for a spin. As soon as we pulled out of the driveway I realized that my life would never be the same. People in the neighboring cars were laughing, smiling, and pointing us out to one another. They were giving me the thumbs-up sign and pounding on the sides of their own cars in an attempt to make contact with us. Peter and I were ecstatic. This was a supreme example of the positive power of acting like a fool, a rolling billboard that shouted out to the people we passed, *"Nothing is that serious! Come on out and have some fun!"*

In the weeks that followed, whenever I left the car in pub-lic I almost always found it surrounded by admiring crowds. Every group seemed to have at least one person who was seized by the irresistible desire to mimic the runners and to stand frozen in front of the car, right fist angled out ahead, left leg kicking behind, smiling delightedly at the cheers and comments from the other onlookers.

The Race Car, as we came to call it, provided an opportunity beyond my wildest expectations for me to make contact with other people, and for total strangers to reach out to me. A man came running up to me as I started to enter the car, and he shook my hand excitedly. "My wife came here to go shopping," he told me. "She took one look at your car and then drove all the way home to get me so that I could see it before it drove away."

Later that same week I prepared to pull out of a parking lot when the parking attendant ambled over to me. "I've been waiting to see who owned this car," he said, looking me over cautiously. "I figured it was either a starving artist or some kind of a mad genius."

Some people who couldn't wait around to meet me would leave notes on the windshield instead. One note I got while I was parked at the college where I was teaching said, "I love your car. If you are not a student in the art department, why not?" Another simply said, "Your car is great! It makes me feel good!"

I mentally prepared myself for someone to have a strongly negative reaction to the Race Car and to unleash a torrent of abuse and contempt on me, but it never happened. The only negative incident, in fact, was a fairly predictable piece of vandalism: one day I returned to the car to find that the woman runner who was leading the race had been snapped off at the ankles. Whether it was coincidence that she was the only runner damaged, or whether she was intentionally destroyed by some outraged male chauvinist I will never know, but my response was an effortless one. I simply moved the woman in the number-seven position up to the number-one spot and re-placed her with one of the spare men from my collection.

As you might imagine, the first time I drove my car to the site of a running race it caused a minor sensation. It made me feel wonderful when a twelve-year-old girl came over to me and said, with tears in her eyes, "I can't believe that you let a woman win the race on top of your car. That is such an inspiration to me that I am going to go out today and run the best race of my life!"

Things came to a total standstill when I went to a car wash. Both the attendants and all the other customers stared open-mouthed as I drove in. They had seen plenty of customized cars in their day, but they had never seen anything like this before. I drove onto the conveyor belt and ran to the end of the wash line as the car emerged from its bath. Everyone else in the place ran along with me. Would the runners survive the attack of the soapy bristles? Would the rubber washers really protect the inside of the car as Peter had promised me, or would the car emerge flooded with water through the holes in the roof? A shout of triumph went up from half a dozen throats as the car emerged, victorious, from its maiden washing. It glistened. It shined. And the runners looked great. My car received its first standing ovation as I drove off to work.

Since I worked on a college campus, it was inevitable that my car would become an object of serious academic study. Classes from the art department came outside to take a look at the Race Car, and anthropology classes examined the car as well. Since historically the gift of the fool is to be a teacher, this particular act of foolishness proved to be of great use to my fellow faculty members, who wished to teach their students about a different way of looking at life.

One of the anthropology professors came by my office to tell me about the field trip his class took to the parking lot to examine the Race Car. "I asked my students, what is the difference between a teenager driving around town in a Trans Am, revving up his engine every time he sees some girls, and you driving around town in this wacky car of yours? The difference is an important one. The teenager is driving around going *Vroom! Vroom!* and what he is saying to people is 'Look at me. This is who I am!' You, on the other hand, are driving around town in your Race Car, but what you are saying to people is 'Look at me. Who are you?' "

22

Play Fair:
Ethics Is
Good Business

In making ethical decisions in an organizational, corporate, or work-group setting, many people seem to believe that profits and ethics do not go hand in hand. "It's a dog-eat-dog world," they say. "You've got to look out for number one." Those who say this are, I think, showing not only that they misunderstand ethics but also that they know very little about dogs. I've been studying dogs for most of my life; I've had a golden retriever who ate broccoli and grapes and a standard poodle who ate Brie, but I've never come across a dog who would even consider eating another dog.

I have given an even more thorough study to ethics than I have to dogs. I am absolutely convinced that ethical behavior is important not only for a healthy personal life but also for a sense of well-being in our lives as workers. I am even more certain that living each day and making each decision as though you are in a dog fight (especially one where the loser gets eaten!) is a very stressful way to live. Not only will you be short on playmates, but you will not be likely to experience much joy or laughter. It is exceedingly difficult to laugh and play when you are always looking over your shoulder to see who is gaining on you or which dog will try to devour you next.

The belief that we must always pursue our own self-interests is known as Ethical Egoism. Most people find this theory far too extreme, and share instead the commonsense view that we *ought* to find some balanced way of being in the world—that both our own interests and the interests of others are important when we make decisions, business or otherwise. Most people recognize that we must consider not only how our decisions affect ourselves, but also how they affect others. If we can agree with this view, then in both our personal and professional lives we are obligated to strive to follow—at the very least—one essential ethical principle; that is, we have to try to play fair. In large measure, I was acknowledging the central importance of this principle twenty-four years ago when I established my own company and called it Playfair. A doctrine of fairness is a key component of almost all modern ethical theories. And in his best-selling book *All I Really Need to Know I Learned in Kindergarten,* Robert Fulghum reminds us that we all were taught the wisdom of this ethical principle long ago as children at play in the school yard.

Many companies, organizations, and individuals are beginning to realize that playing fair is the right thing to do in the world of work and business. It's desirable not only because it makes us feel good about ourselves, but also because it makes good business sense. Chairman and chief executive officer of Levi Strauss & Co. Robert D. Haas has said that a corporation should be an "ethical creature." He argues that there is clearly a connection between ethical action and business success. Timothy Price, president of business markets at MCI, points out that ethics in business—playing fair—ultimately leads to creativity, an essential element of continued profitability.

The list of leaders who have recognized the relationship between ethics and earnings grows daily. The message is becoming crystal clear: playing fair with employees, customers, and one another is good business.

What, then, is the best way to ensure that we are playing fair? In truth, it isn't always easy to tell if we are behaving ethically. I think the best direction I have ever received in this regard was when I had the good fortune of participating in a small discussion with the Fourteenth Dalai Lama of Tibet. I found him to be a gentle and compassionate man, and I was deeply impressed by both his sincerity and his humor. I felt a very clear sense of this great man's presence and, even more important perhaps, I felt that here was a person who lived what he believed. In our meeting, the simple criteria that he offered for the rightness of an act was this: an act is good and right if it is performed with a right heart.

"But Your Holiness," several of the theologians and philosophers in attendance protested, "what if the intentions are good but the results of the act are clearly bad?"

"It is the rightness of the heart that matters, not the consequences of the act," he maintained.

"But Your Holiness, what if one thinks he is acting with a good heart but continually has bad results?"

"In that case," he replied, "one needs to take a most careful look at one's heart."

I think that when we take a close look sometimes our right heart will tell us that we can't always be focused on the bottom line. We can't have our attention solely fixed on what good will come to us personally. Sure, it will still be important to do a cost/benefit analysis. Of course, we will still try to ensure corporate well-being and our own well-being within the organization as well. However, when our heart is right, we won't always be looking at dollars—at least not in the short term. When we have a right heart we won't pursue our own needs so exclusively that we are willing to step on others or stab them in the back. Rather, we will see our coworkers the same way we long ago saw our childhood playmates—as people we want to help and with whom we want to cooperate.

In the final analysis, I'm not sure if we can ever improve on that way of being with one another. As we go about our business with employees, customers, suppliers, and coworkers, what more can we ask of ourselves than that we choose our actions with a right heart? When you want to know what to do in a problematic situation, take a close look at your heart. If your heart is right, then you know that you are playing fair.

II

Turn Problems into Opportunities

23

Change the Way
You View the World

Barry Merkin is a turnaround specialist who was brought in as the president of Dresher, Inc., the nation's largest manufacturer of brass beds. On his first day at the company, Barry gathered all the employees together for a meeting so he could share his philosophy of business with them. In an attempt to build up the sagging morale at the plant, he told the assembled employees that they should view their problem areas as "opportunities to help the company get back on its feet." He said he didn't want to hear any of them complaining about problems anymore. "From now on in this company, there are no more problems—there are only opportunities!"

Later that afternoon Barry heard sirens wailing nearby, and looking out his window, he saw the flashing lights of emergency vehicles heading down to the loading dock. Concerned, he called down to the foreman and asked what the commotion was all about. "Well, Mr. Merkin," replied the foreman thoughtfully, "it seems we've got quite a medical opportunity down here at the dock!"

The lesson Barry Merkin learned is an important one: turning problems into opportunities involves more than just a change in terminology—it involves a change in the way we view the world. The reason someone views a particular event as a problem is not inherent in the event itself. Rather, it is caused by one's *reaction* to the given event.

To put it simply, both problems and opportunities exist only in your mind. The same situation that looks like a problem to one person can look like an opportunity to someone else. The best illustration of this is the famous sales-training story about an Australian sales manager who sends two salespeople deep into the outback to sells shoes to the Aborigines. The two salespeople have been instructed to telegram after a week to report on their progress. On the appointed day the first salesman wires back, HOPELESS. AM RETURNING HOME ON NEXT TRAIN. THE PEOPLE DON'T EVEN WEAR SHOES OUT HERE! Discouraged, the sales manager turns to the next telegram, which reads, A GOLD MINE! SEND MORE SAMPLES AT ONCE. THE PEOPLE DON'T EVEN WEAR SHOES OUT HERE!

The fundamental way you view the world has a profound effect on whether you see problems or opportunities arising in your life. Think, for example, about the last time you saw an infant crawl into a room filled with grown-ups. Instantly, everybody stopped what they were doing to focus on the baby. They started laughing and smiling and talking baby talk. No matter what had been going on before, the room was transformed into a place of delight by the baby's arrival.

When was the last time you walked into a group of people and had that kind of effect on them?

Obviously, this is not a question of power—I'm not suggesting that an infant is more powerful than you are. It is, however, an excellent example of how your worldview can influence what happens to you. An infant, by and large, imagines herself to be surrounded by a benevolent universe that is filled with all sorts of giant, happy, smiling creatures whose main intention seems to be to make her happy. And so she finds herself in a world filled with opportunities.

Most adults, on the other hand, are taught that it's a highly competitive world out there, that there aren't enough material goods to go around, and that you had better carve out your slice of the pie and defend it against all comers before there's none left for you. And so you find yourself in a world filled with problems.

Can you learn to turn your problems into opportunities? You certainly can. Would you rather live in a world filled with problems, or a world filled with opportunities? The choice is yours.

24

See the Flowers
in the Garbage

One day I was riding in a car driven by my friend Steve when we noticed another car in the distance, its roof entirely covered with all kinds of junk and debris that flew off in all directions as it approached us. "Isn't that disgusting?" he commented, pointing to the approaching vehicle. "You'd think people would take a little more pride in the way their cars look."

As we got closer to the car in question, however, we realized that what we had taken for junk and debris was actually flower petals. The car had evidently been parked overnight underneath a flowering tree, which had deposited a layer of petals all over the roof. "Whoops!" remarked Steve. "Forget what I just said!"

Just the week before I had been reading a book by Zen master Thich Nhat Hanh, in which he had been talking about the interrelatedness of all life. When he looked deeply into a flower, he wrote, he could already see it dying and decomposing and returning to the earth. Likewise, when he looked into a pile of garbage, he could see the seeds of life in it, and could envision it turning into the blooming flower that it someday would be. I shared my memory of that passage with Steve, and we talked about the nature of reality and illusion. "Well, maybe I wasn't so wrong after all," he said after a while.

It can be hard to tell, in the moment when it's happening, whether an event is garbage or flowers. Because in the long run it's probably both of them. We see a snapshot of a young woman completely immersed in waves, and we think, "The poor woman is drowning." But if we could see the next snapshot in the sequence, we would see her body shooting into the air on the far side of the wave, and we would realize, "Oh, she's bodysurfing. She's diving through the waves." Without the element of time, without the long view, our understanding of the events in our lives can be only snapshots—poorly photographed, out-of-focus snapshots at that. We can only guess whether we are looking at flowers or garbage, or even garbage turning into flowers.

Shakespearean actor Fran deLeon ("Don't call me an actress!" cautions Fran. "Would you call a female doctor a doctress? Or a female lawyer a lawyeress?"), like many struggling actors, had to take a number of different jobs to support herself while she was waiting for her big break in the theater. One time she signed up to be Barney the dinosaur to perform magic tricks at kids' parties. "Of course the problem was that I'm five feet tall, and the Barney costume was designed for someone six feet tall," Fran remembers. "So Barney's legs all ended in a big bunch of material covering my feet, and I had to stumble around in this giant's costume, trying to peer through this enormous purple Barney head, while I was attempting to do magic tricks for the kids."

One of Barney's best magic tricks was that he opens a pan

and shows that it's empty. The pan has a false bottom, however, and the next time Barney opens up the pan, a live rabbit appears. "The first time I tried this, it was a big hit with all the kids. They all started applauding and yelling and laughing—it was the greatest thing they had ever seen. What the producer forgot to tell me, however, was that this was a completely untrained rabbit. The rabbit got spooked by all the noise, it was terrified of the kids, and so it climbed up Barney's costume and in through one of the eyeholes, and it disappeared from sight, poking around inside the costume, looking for someplace to hide.

"Now, this completely freaked me, to have the rabbit climbing all around inside my costume, and so I ran out of the room so I could get out of the costume and free the rabbit. The kids, however, were completely traumatized by the whole thing, and I could hear them hysterically crying and sobbing back in the room where I had left them, screaming out, 'Barney ate the rabbit! Barney ate the rabbit!' "

Several weeks later Fran got a call to be Zippy the Mailbox for a couple of hours at a corporate convention. The costume was about four feet six inches tall, and it hung very low off Fran's five-foot frame. She had to wear black tights and big tennis shoes, and the costume included Mickey Mouse hands with three fingers and a thumb. Fran placed herself under the box with a shoulder harness and walked around handing out flyers for her client, which was made doubly difficult because of the Mickey Mouse gloves.

As Fran walked around the exhibit hall, conventioneers would approach the mailbox and say, "Is that a real person in there, or are you a midget?" After a while they'd get a little more raucous and start banging on the mailbox, saying things like "Got any mail for me?" or "Special delivery!" or "Check's in the mail!" "The banging would sound really loud inside the costume," recalls Fran, "and it would really hurt!"

After taking a few breaks and feeling more and more sorry for herself, Fran started walking around the exhibit hall reciting to herself the balcony monologue from *Romeo and Juliet*. She knew no one could hear her voice from within the mailbox. As she walked by a mirror Fran caught sight of herself and realized how ridiculous she looked. "I understood why people were banging on the mailbox, because I was such a pathetic sight," she admitted.

Fran looked straight ahead and saw Zippy staring back at her mockingly in the mirror. She held out the Mickey Mouse hands imploringly, as if to reassure herself about what was real and what was not, and shouted back to her image in the mirror, "I'm an actor! I'm an actor!"

"I felt really bad that people couldn't see the flesh-and-blood actor under the costume, but I had to believe in myself. I knew that someday I would be able to look in the mirror and see my real face looking back saying, 'I'm an actor!' "

Seven years later, things came full circle when Fran played Juliet at the Los Angeles Theater Center, a production seen by more than seventy-five hundred people during its run. "The person who wore the clownish mailbox was the same person who wore Juliet's beautiful gown," says Fran. "I was the same person inside both costumes, even though nobody else could see it."

Even though the production of *Romeo and Juliet* was very successful, there were still some occasions when the audience didn't respond the way Fran had hoped. "But just like in the Zippy the Mailbox days, I didn't lose faith in my ability and commitment. And so I said the same words to myself over and over again in those difficult moments: 'I'm an actor! I'm an actor!'

"And then I thought, 'And at least I'm not playing Zippy the Mailbox anymore!' "

We can't have fun and play in our lives all the time. Sometimes our interactions with other people bring us pain; sometimes life needs to hit us over the head with a frying pan in order for us to learn what we need to learn. But even in those times of pain, it can be comforting to remember that life is cyclical and that things always change. Spring follows winter, sunrise follows sunset, and the energy of our days is not possible without the rest periods of our nights.

We all have days when we look in the mirror and see our own equivalent of Zippy the Mailbox staring back at us. There will be times that we get so mired in the garbage that we forget what flowers even look like. But just because we are covered in garbage at any given moment doesn't mean that our lives are garbage. It just means that the flowers haven't arrived yet.

A difficult thing to remember is that even if life is not sending you any flowers at this very moment, you can always send a delivery to yourself. You can always find a way to give yourself a little treat in times of adversity, as a reminder of the flowers soon to come. You can go out to the movies, you can take a walk in the park, you can play fetch with a dog, you can invite a friend over for a special dinner, you can call up the florist and send a love note home to yourself.

Hey, I think I hear the doorbell ringing right now! Don't forget to act surprised when the bouquet arrives.

Secrets of
Stress Reduction
—— Part I:
Don't Choose Stress

I've been spending way too much time lately at O'Hare International Airport in Chicago, which is considered by many people to be the stress epicenter of the known universe. One evening I was standing in line to buy a ticket to Dallas, where I was scheduled to give a speech the next day. The woman in front of me was also trying to buy a ticket to Dallas, but she was having some sort of trouble, and so the ticket agent finally asked her to step aside while he took care of the rest of us.

Ten minutes later I spotted the same woman walking up to the Dallas gate. She was visibly upset, and as soon as she saw me she walked right over to where I was standing. In an attempt to be friendly, I asked her if she had straightened out her ticket, and she told me that no, she hadn't. In a halting voice she explained that she had been mugged the night before and had lost her wallet and credit

cards. So she had telephoned her uncle in Texas, and he had ordered her a prepaid ticket. The problem was that the airline
computer showed her reservation on the Dallas flight, but it
didn't show that her ticket had been paid for.

"I don't know what to do," she said to me in despair. "This
is the last flight of the night to Dallas. I guess I'll have to stay
in the airport overnight, and I'll call my uncle in the morning
and have him go over to his travel agent and straighten it all
out."

At this point two conflicting thoughts occurred to me. The
first was "Here is a poor stranded woman. I can help her out,
buy her a ticket, and she can pay me back when we get to Dallas." The second, more powerful thought was "Here is a con
artist trying to rip me off for an airplane ticket. There is no way
I'm going to fall for that one!"

Now, it so happens that during my college days I worked
one summer as a redcap in the Port Authority Bus Terminal in
New York City, and I met all sorts of con artists and saw all sorts
of scams in action. I even got to be good friends with one of the
veteran con artists, a guy whose pitch was "I just need two
more bucks to get a ticket back to Buffalo. Can you help me
out, pal?" He made more money than I did, and by the end of
the summer he probably could have purchased a limo and
driven back to Buffalo in style. Except, of course, that he had
no intention of going to Buffalo.

So I considered myself a pretty good judge of character, a
seasoned veteran when it came to sniffing out scams. As I
talked with this woman for a few more minutes, something
melted inside of me. I thought to myself, "This woman needs
my help; there's no way she's a con artist." So I said to her,
"Don't worry, you don't need to sleep in the terminal overnight.
Come on, I'll buy you a ticket, and you can pay me back when
we get to Dallas."

We walked over to the ticket counter together, and that's what really clinched it for me. It turned out that she had a discount reservation for the flight. Instead of setting me back the $250 I had just paid for my own ticket, her ticket only cost me $110. We got seats next to each other on the plane, and she told me all about her life in Dallas and her job with Texas Instruments. I had to prepare some notes for my talk the next day, so I couldn't spend as much time with her as I wanted to. But she was truly delightful company, and I knew I had made the right choice. We parted amiably at the baggage claim, and she promised to come by my hotel the next morning at nine o'clock sharp with a check for me. I felt great about my generous gesture to my newfound friend.

Nine o'clock the next morning arrived, and she didn't show up. I had to go off to the convention center to give my presentation, and when I checked back at my hotel later in the day, there still was no message from her. "Are you sure there's nothing for me?" I asked the front desk clerk, certain that there had been some sort of mistake. "No messages, no envelopes, no checks?"

By the next morning when there was still no word from her, I was starting to get worried. So I searched around for the scrap of paper on which she had written her phone number. I carefully dialed the number, hoping against hope that I was not dialing the number for the time and temperature in Dallas. The phone rang for a long time, and I broke into a cold sweat. But then someone answered, "Good morning, Texas Instruments!" and I breathed a sigh of relief, my faith in humanity restored. I knew there was going to be a reasonable explanation for the fact that I hadn't received the money yet. I asked for my friend's extension, but there was no such extension. I asked for her by name, and the operator told me there was no such person working there.

With a sinking feeling, I realized that I had just been taken for $110 by a professional scam artist.

My first reaction was fury and fantasies of intense revenge. I would take the next month off from work and camp out at O'Hare. I would find that woman, and I would stomp her into the ground. I would take all her money, so the next time she told somebody she had been mugged, she would be telling the truth. I would set fire to her driver's license. I would call the airport police, the state police, the FBI, and Interpol. I didn't even know what Interpol was, but I knew it was necessary for this case.

Finally, I realized—wait a minute! This is exactly what I always teach people not to do. The human imagination is very powerful, and reliving a stressful situation over and over again in the memory can be as harmful to your health as actually undergoing the initial stress reaction. How many times have we seen two of our friends in identical "stressful" situations, and watched one of them fall to pieces while the other one moves beautifully through her life? The difference lies in the way each person internalizes that situation, the way she interprets what is happening to her. Stress is not inherent in any one particular event; it's a part of your reaction to the event.

In other words, stress is all in your mind.

I knew that the more I daydreamed about wreaking revenge on my tormentor, the more I focused on negative thoughts, the more damage I was doing to myself. As long as I kept thinking about the past, which I couldn't control, I was continually tormenting myself without having any effect whatsoever on the woman who had ripped me off. If there is any justice in this universe, then she'll get hers, but the only punishing that I was doing was to the victim—me.

So I took a deep breath, calmed myself down, and asked myself, "Okay, Mr. Stress Management Consultant, what is another way that you can look at this situation so it won't drive you crazy? What's another version of this reality? How can you put this behind you and get back into the game?"

After I thought about it for a while, I suddenly realized that I had just witnessed one of the great theatrical performances of all time. This woman deserved an Oscar!

Of course I don't usually pay $110 a ticket when I go to the theater.

But I don't usually get to sit that close, either!

Secrets of Stress Reduction ——— Part II: Learn to Reframe Life's Little Upsets

Even when we understand the strategy of dealing with stressful situations, all the techniques in the world are easy to forget in the heat of the moment. The key is to remember that stressful things don't just happen to us: we have to choose them. Stress is always a choice.

That is not to say that painful and grievous situations do not exist in our lives. Of course they do. But each of us reacts differently to those situations. We can choose how we will react. It is up to us to create our own emotional reality, and in any given situation there are as many different realities as there are ways to look at the situation. There is no emotional reality outside of what happens in our own minds.

When you're in the grip of a stressful situation, you feel your stomach muscles begin to tighten, and at that moment you have a choice. You can be seized with the tension of the stressful moment, or you can take a deep breath and ask yourself, "What is another way that I can look at this situation so it won't seem quite so stressful for me? What is another perspective I can take on these events? What is an alternate reality I can enter right now, so I won't be tearing myself to pieces over this?"

This technique is called reframing. The most difficult thing to do during a stressful situation is to remember that what is causing you to feel stress is a version of reality, not reality itself. Remember to take a deep breath, let your mind disengage from the pain you are feeling in the moment, and begin the search for an alternative perspective. This engages the part of your brain that looks for creative solutions, and the mere act of creative thinking can in itself provide an antidote to stress.

For practice, select two or three situations that were negative or unpleasant for you in the past month. They can be things that were really insignificant, like the time another driver flipped you the bird while you were driving to work. Perhaps now you realize that you invested lots of unnecessary energy replaying the event over and over in your mind. Use your imagination to create and then write down as many positive, lighthearted responses to the situation as you can. Don't be afraid to be outrageous! See if you can create a possibility that will make you laugh out loud.

When you succeed in reframing a stressful situation, the tension often goes right out of it, and you often find yourself laughing in relief. How often have you heard someone say "Someday I know I'm going to look back at all this and laugh"? The question that you need to ask yourself in all these reframable situations is "Why wait? Let's laugh at it now!"

27

Secrets of Stress Reduction — Part III: Rethink Difficult Situations

In my early years after entering the job market, I never had much money. So I adopted a policy about automobiles that most of my friends found somewhat unusual: I made it a point never to pay more than five hundred dollars for a car. That way, I would never have unreasonable expectations about the car and what it could do for me. After all, only a fool would expect a five-hundred-dollar car to start and run properly. At the same time, I knew lots of people who paid thirty or even fifty thousand dollars for their cars. They got very upset when they had car trouble, because for that kind of money they expected to have a machine that performs perfectly.

With my track record of mechanical catastrophes, I knew that I would be begging for trouble if I had too many positive expectations about my automobile. So the way I had it framed, my relationship to cars was a big game. One of the rules of the game was this: when my car had a serious breakdown, I just junked it and bought another one. Why choose stress?

That's not to say I didn't get very attached to my cars, because I did. In fact, I always named them, and in the course of this book you'll read several stories involving the old junkers that have owned me over the years. One of these experiences showed me quite clearly that rethinking my attitude toward a situation can determine for me whether the situation is ultimately negative or positive.

During the time when I was driving Opie, my old Buick Opal, I had a lot of trouble keeping up with my car keys. I could never find them when I needed them, until I figured out that I wouldn't ever lose them if I always left them where they belonged—in the ignition. My friends warned me that someday I was going to get my car stolen this way. I would laugh at them and say, "Do you really think someone would steal this old car? Besides, no one would make it more than three blocks away, because you have to know a lot of special tricks to drive my car." I felt confident that my car was safe. Then one morning I went out to drive to work and, lo and behold, someone had stolen my car keys.

When I told my friends that my keys had been stolen, they all wanted to know what I planned to do about it. Well, what could I do? I certainly couldn't call the police and report some stolen keys! So I said I'd just have to wait until the thief came back and tried to get the car itself. In an attempt to look on the bright side, I told myself that I could use some exercise, and it was probably a good time to start riding my bicycle to work.

Two weeks later, a group of my friends met at my house to go for a run. Since the key theft, the only use I'd been able to find for my old car was as a stretching post before running. As we went outside to stretch against the car I realized that the key thief had been upgraded to car thief—Opie was missing.

My friends excitedly offered me their opinions of what I should do next, and I told them that we had come together for a run, and I was still planning to go for a run; we could figure out the next step after we returned. Why ruin the whole afternoon?

We hadn't gone more than three blocks when we came across Opie, pulled in catywampus to the curb. The thief had obviously experienced some car problems, as I knew he would. The keys, however, were still not in the ignition. I thought perhaps the thief had thrown the keys away in frustration, so my friends and I got down on our hands and knees and combed the area looking for them, but no luck. Friends they truly were, however, since they helped me push old Opie back up to the front of my house before we continued our run.

As I ran, I wondered how I might best respond to this situation. Could I rethink it into something playful? I realized that if I called and reported the incident to the police, nothing positive would happen. That's not to suggest anything negative about the police, I was just being realistic. They'd come out to my house, take down the pertinent information, and file a stolen-car report. I would call a locksmith, pay fifty or seventy-five dollars for a new ignition and key, and the case would be closed.

I tried to think of every possible alternative, every stress-free way I could turn the incident into a game. Later I sat down at my typewriter and wrote the car thief the following letter:

Dear Car Thief,

I don't mind you borrowing my car once in a while. However, I would appreciate it if you would be so kind as to leave the keys in the car when you're not using it so that I can use it. Furthermore, if you will come up and knock on my door, I'll teach you how to drive the car so that next time you can make it more than three blocks.

I signed the letter, then fastened it to the car by rolling the car window up with the letter on top of it, writing facing out.

The next morning, as I roared out of the driveway on my bicycle, I glanced over at the letter and saw to my great delight that the car thief had written a reply. I found the following response scrawled beneath my own typewritten letter:

> *I think you are crazy. Why would you let your car be my car? Not only are you crazy, you are also blind. The keys are in the ignition and they have been there all along.*

Indeed, the keys were right back in the ignition where they belonged!

I share this story with you to demonstrate an essential element in rethinking a problem situation. I suppose I could have pounded myself over the head for being so stupid as to leave my keys in the car and let my car get stolen, but to what end? The car was stolen; that was a simple fact. If I was going to get on with life as game, then I needed to start with the given (i.e., the car is stolen, too late to take the keys out now), and then see how many playful, positive possibilities I could create to remedy that fact. Then, after exhausting the possibilities, I could choose the one I wanted to put into action.

One reason we all tend to be self-limiting is that we feel more secure and more in control of an unfamiliar situation if we are locked in to a familiar, standard, predictable way of responding to that situation. But that is not the only way to be in control of what happens to you. When you rethink situations, then you see new possibilities for your life. When you see possibilities, then you realize you always have choices and options. When you make a choice, then you feel in control. When you feel in control, then you feel secure. For that reason, rethinking is one of the most empowering activities you can undertake. In the long run, you will probably reject more than 99 percent of the possibilities you come up with, but just think of all the fun you can have along the way, letting your imagination run wild.

28

Remember the Democratic Character of Life

Although it is sometimes easy to forget, human life has a democratic character. As ancient wisdom has always taught us, all humans are of the nature to grow old. We are all of the nature to become sick. All of us must die. Of course, life is democratic in other, more positive ways. For example, we can all experience happiness, joy, and a sense of meaning.

Recognizing life's democratic character is important, for it can teach us that, in the final analysis, no one is more or less important than anyone else. This helps us to remember not to take ourselves too seriously.

We have a tendency to forget the democratic character of life in two ways, both of which can have a profound effect upon our professional and personal lives. First, we make the mistake of becoming filled with the idea of our own importance, believing that our positions, our possessions, our professions, our profiles make us more valuable than other people. This is the mistake my mother used to call false pride and the early Greeks called hubris.

Conversely, we can make the mistake of becoming mired in low self-esteem, believing that somehow another person is more important than we are. We are led into both mistakes by indulging ourselves too much in the practice of comparing ourselves with others, focusing on strange ideas like "better than" or "worse than."

The well-known Greek myth of Icarus and his father, Daedalus, makes the point about these two mistakes in an interesting and creative way. In order to escape from imprisonment on a Greek island, Daedalus fashions artificial wings made of feathers and wax for himself and his son. Before they take flight, Daedalus warns Icarus not to fly too high, for if he does, the sun will melt the wax and he will crash into the sea. But the part of the story that always struck me, and that many people tend to forget, is that he also warns him not to fly too low, for if he flies too low the mist from the sea will soak the feathers and he will crash. As the story goes, once they were airborne Icarus was filled with pride about his ability to fly. So he began to soar higher and higher until the wax was melted and he crashed into the sea.

Many Greek myths warn about overweening pride; however, it is important to remember that this myth also warns that flying too low—that is, not thinking enough of yourself—leads to a crash as well. In my experience people are just as likely, if not more likely, to crash and burn by flying too low than by flying too high. We invite great unhappiness and low morale into our lives by thinking that other people are more important than we are.

I've been much more comfortable in my life since I realized that in any real or ultimate sense, there is no one more or less important than I am. I still remember very clearly the day that lesson came home to roost. For many years Margaret Mead had been a heroine to me. I admired her work with the South Sea peoples, her position as the world's most famous anthropologist, and especially the fact that she had accomplished this in the face of overwhelming prejudice against anthropologists who happened to be women.

You can imagine my excitement when she was invited to give a speech in my town, and I learned that I was going to be the lucky individual who would be picking her up at the airport. I had met some "important" people before; however, on none of those occasions was I fazed in the slightest. But I felt so small next to the great Margaret Mead that I worried for days about meeting her.

Of course, some part of my concern was because I was driving to the airport to pick her up in *my* car—the aforementioned Opie. On the way to the airport I uttered a few prayers regarding my mission. After all, Opie did have problems enough to elicit some heartfelt prayers. To give you an idea of the high-quality automobile I was driving back in those days, let me explain that when I turned to the right, the driver-side door came open. And when I turned to the left, the horn honked.

To further fill my mind with doubts, I was carrying the memory of the time that I picked up NASA astronaut Brian Leahy at the airport. On that memorable occasion I couldn't get Opie started, and Brian ended up pushing me all over the parking lot while I sat behind the wheel popping the clutch and urging the car into action. I'm not so sure that an astronaut who was both a highly trained pilot and a technological wizard could fully appreciate the humor in that situation. Even today, when I think about this man—who was accustomed to traveling in state-of-the-art, hundred-million-dollar vehicles—first pushing and then riding in a vehicle like Opie, I shake my head in amazement.

As I rode to the airport, however, the thought of my heroine Margaret Mead having to push my car to get it started didn't strike me as the least bit funny. I began to think of every awful thing that could possibly go wrong. Though I had seen her picture many times, I even wondered as I stood weak-kneed and sweaty-palmed in the waiting area, "What if I don't recognize her?"

Very quickly my fears of not recognizing her were put to rest, while my overall anxieties about meeting the great Dr. Mead were greatly increased. A very tiny woman came walking off the plane wearing a flowered muumuu and carrying a huge shepherd's staff. She later explained to me that friends had given her the staff to assist her in walking. To me, however, it seemed as if Moses or perhaps God herself had just disembarked from American Airlines.

So, prepared for the worst and with all the confidence of a worm, I picked up the queen's luggage and headed for the coach, which was likely to become a pumpkin at any moment. I helped Dr. Mead into the passenger's seat and muttered a few more prayers to myself as I loaded her luggage and staff into the backseat. When I got into the car I looked over and noticed that she was fishing around in the seat as though she was looking for something. I asked if there was a problem, and she said that she was looking for the seat belt. This was well before there were any seat belt laws, and I had no idea if Opie even had a seat belt for the passenger side. So as my anxiety increased, I jumped out of the car and ran around to the other side to help in the search.

As I fished around under the seat with her, I remarked that I wasn't too sure that the car even had a seat belt. She looked at me very seriously and said, "Young man, are you sure that this is your car?"

In that instant, there was an incredible leveling that took place between the great one and the insignificant one. The moment is etched in my memory. I briefly surveyed my beat-up old rattletrap, then looked her squarely in the eye. "Dr. Mead," I said, "if I were going to borrow a car to come pick you up, do you think I would borrow *this* car?"

I realized then that even great geniuses could ask very stupid questions. I saw clearly that behind all of her degrees, fame, and accomplishment stood Margaret Mead, human being. Once I realized that, we became fast friends. I was able to meet her as human being to human being. We had great fun together for the rest of the day and evening, and after her speech that night, we talked in her hotel room long into the night on every topic from divorce to dancing.

I still admire her and respect her greatly, but I also know that she was one of us—no more and no less important than any other human being. Whenever I start to forget that lesson and begin to believe that one person is more important than another, or even worse, that I am more important than anyone else, I try to remember this story. If all else fails, then I think of the wonderful quote of the sixteenth-century essayist Michel de Montaigne: "The highest king on the highest throne still sits upon his own arse."

In the world of business we often forget that no one is more or less important than anyone else. This happens most frequently in large organizations, which tend to emphasize hierarchy rather than democracy. Vice presidents and directors can begin to fly far too close to the sun, believing that they are somehow special. Nonmanagement employees in turn may fly too low and let their self-esteem be negatively affected by the fact that they perceive themselves as the bottom figure on the corporate totem pole. This, of course, is not good for anyone's ability to laugh and play on the job. Even worse, it can be detrimental to the survival of the organization, because the resulting low morale invariably leads to lower productivity.

One of the fundamental keys to taking ourselves lightly, whether at work or in our personal lives, is to remember the democratic character of life. We must remember that no matter how important or unimportant another person may seem, ultimately "importance" is nothing but an illusion. Those who can see through the illusion will wind up having the last laugh.

Turn Fights into Frolics
———— Part I: Crack an Egg on Your Head

During my years in graduate school, I was in love with a woman named Susan. Like any couple, we had our arguments and disagreements, and we each did our share of yelling and screaming, slamming doors and stomping around the house.

One night we were arguing in the kitchen. I was so angry that I had convinced myself that this argument had nothing to do with my sadness or any of my hurt feelings—this one was about right and wrong. I was right, and she was wrong. She had hurt me, and I wanted to hurt her back. I yelled. I screamed. I shot poisonous vapors out of my eyes. And Susan was hooked into this argument in a big way. She was not about to back down. She shouted back at me with an ever-increasing anger.

In my most demented fantasies I wanted to slam her against the refrigerator, or, even better, to slam the refrigerator against her. We glared at each other with undisguised fury, and we screamed without ever listening to each other. The little voice of sanity inside my head told me to calm down, to remember that Susan was the woman I loved, and I told that voice to shut up and mind its own business. Then, without thinking, I suddenly reached out for an egg carton that was sitting on the counter. On a sudden impulse I opened up the carton, pulled out an egg, and clutched it tight in my trembling hand.

Without missing a beat, staring directly at Susan with a menacing grimace on my face, I smashed the egg on my head.

Susan was stopped dead in her tracks, and I could see her fierce gaze start to waver momentarily, as the slightest hint of panic crept into her eyes. I continued to send her my most hostile and unforgiving looks, but then the egg yolk started dripping down my nose. It was impossible for either of us to keep a straight face, and we both burst out laughing hysterically. Susan grabbed a dish towel to wipe me off, and I gave her an egg-stained kiss.

I had inadvertently stumbled onto one of the great secrets of maintaining a life of laughter and play in the face of great emotional turmoil: be unpredictable, and act like a fool. In the middle of an argument, do the thing you are least likely to do. Whatever the logical way to proceed may be, do exactly the opposite, especially if it makes you look foolish. This technique has three great advantages: 1. It gets your partner's immediate attention; 2. It turns your own attention in a creative direction, rather than an aggressive one; and 3. It disorients both of you for the moment, which creates a temporary hiatus from the emotional charge of the argument, during which time you can escape from its tyrannical grip.

In the same way that two negative numbers multiplied together magically create a positive number, so two seemingly negative gestures can sometimes lead to a positive result. There is no better time to act the fool than in the middle of a heated argument. So the next time you are having an argument at home, head right for the kitchen. If you are in the middle of a fight worthy of the name, your partner will certainly follow you on your journey toward the refrigerator, hurling insults at your retreating back all the way. Once you are safely ensconced in the kitchen, you can use your own sense of dramatic timing to reach for the egg at the moment of maximum impact.

I guarantee you that this unexpected gesture of self-mutilation will put an immediate end to any argument and will leave both of you feeling closer to each other. Any urge toward physical violence you may have experienced will be totally satisfied, and you will feel a madcap glee take over your mind as the rage quickly drains out of you.

The only problem is that when you are feeling angry and self-righteous you may not *want* to put an end to the argument, and you may not *want* to feel closer to your partner, especially if you think you've been wronged. There will come a time when you are not going to want to listen to your own inner voice urging you to calm down, and you are certainly not going to want to listen to my voice urging you to do something unpredictable and foolish. But you can do it. I know you can.

How many times have you been in an argument with someone you loved, and then, after it was all over, you found yourself apologizing and saying you were sorry, and wishing that it had never happened? As a veteran of too many ridiculous arguments over the years, I have learned the hard way that most arguments are misguided pleas for attention and affection. We feel hurt, we feel unloved, and so we start a fight. But most of the time we don't really want to fight at all—just the opposite, in fact: we want to feel loved.

I know you won't feel like doing it, but next time you are in the middle of a heated domestic battle, do yourself a favor and go for the egg. After a few short weeks of doing this, as soon as you start to head for the kitchen the two of you will both start laughing and it will be impossible to carry out a serious argument. Your partner will be pleading with you, "Oh, no, not the egg again, anything but the egg!"

And if you are nowhere near the house, or you are all out of eggs, don't worry, you can find a way to be unpredictable and foolish almost anywhere. What you are really doing is stepping out of your own sense of self-righteousness and, instead, making a grandiose acknowledgment of your own vulnerability. You impulsively create a moment of distance and perspective on the argument that reminds the two of you that the person you feel like you hate is actually someone you love, and someone who loves you as well. It is that knowledge that can help you bring even the most hopeless and angry battles to a loving, upbeat conclusion.

Turn Fights into Frolics
Part II: Be Creative with Your Arguments

I know that there are a number of readers who are thinking, "You must be totally insane if you are suggesting that I crack an egg on my head! There is no way in the world that I would do that. And I'm not exactly thrilled to hear that you did it to your own head, either!"

It is not the cracking of eggs against heads that is important here, but the idea that a conscious, loving relationship between two people is possible to achieve. You and your partner can agree in advance that you are likely to find yourself in heated arguments and that you want to do your best to resolve those arguments as rapidly as possible. If you can turn your arguments into a game, then you are well on the way to turning your fights into frolics. But first you have to agree on the rules of the game.

The first step is to acknowledge that anytime there is intimate communication between two people there is likely to be some miscommunication as well. Whenever two people are in a loving relationship they are likely to feel vulnerable to each other, and sooner or later they are certain to hurt each other, intentionally or unintentionally.

The idea of cracking an egg on your head is an attempt to create a ritual that both partners can participate in, to remind each other of the love that exists beyond the aggravation of the moment. The egg is a signpost that says, "Hey, we don't want to be acting like this—we really care about each other, remember?" Cracking the egg is an attempt to lighten up the inevitable hurt that comes with being vulnerable, but there are certainly many other ways of approaching that same problem in a lighthearted way. You and your partner can make up your own ritual, one that feels comfortable for you.

The important thing is that you and your partner agree in advance on a signal that will remind you that although in the heat of the moment it feels as if you are living with the most horrible monster in the world, underneath it all you really love each other. So you make a pledge to each other that this signal takes absolute priority and must be honored at all times.

My friends Amo and Shelley Tarnoff, for example, found that the best way for them to resolve their disagreements was to set up a system where only one of them can talk at a time, while the other one can only listen, without responding. Then, after three minutes, they switch the roles of speaker (or screamer) and listener. And they keep switching back and forth every three minutes until each of them can begin to hear what the other one is saying and their differences can be resolved.

So Amo and Shelley made a firm agreement that when either one of them said, "Listening mode!" they would immediately stop fighting and move into this method of resolving their differences, regardless of whether they wanted to at the time or not. After they had mastered listening mode, they moved on to a variation they call writing mode. When either one of them calls out, "Writing mode!" in the middle of an argument, they both have to instantly abandon all speech, grab pen and paper, and dash off furious notes to each other. Their rule is, they can keep fighting viciously, but they have to do it in writing. Then they slam their ferocious notes down on the table, and each reads the other's with a look of complete disbelief, then dramatically tears it up. Then they write back angry responses. After a few minutes of scribbled tirades, contemptuous looks, and broken pencil points, they run out of steam. The first words they are allowed to say out loud to each other are, "I'm sorry, honey."

Amo and Shelley have brainstormed all sorts of different fun ways to transform their arguments. One time they decided that in the middle of any argument either of them could say, "Switch clothes!" and they would immediately have to put on each other's clothes. "How could I stay angry with him when I saw him all dressed up in my clothes?" asked Shelley. "My only regret is that I wasn't wearing an evening gown at the time!"

Although my friend Fran was unable to attend my wedding, she did send along a wonderful idea as a gift for us newlyweds. She instructed Geneen and me to set up a table off to one side of the room at our wedding reception. On the table were placed a large manila envelope, a selection of pens, and some writing paper. We then asked the wedding guests to write suggestions for things we could do whenever (as was bound to happen sometime) we got into some Big Arguments. The idea was that sometime in the future, whenever we found ourselves in an unmanageable fight, we would reach into the envelope, pull out one of the sets of instructions from our friends, and do whatever it said.

After the wedding we put the envelope in a desk drawer for handy access, and then we promptly forgot all about it. Several months later, we were in the middle of a big fight. Blanche, our enormously overweight cat, was continuing to gain weight, even though he had been put on a strict diet by his veterinarian. Geneen was extremely concerned about the big guy's health, and she suspected that I had been overfeeding him. This was true. Blanche would catch me alone in the kitchen and would go through an elaborate routine designed to soften me up. First he would let out the most mournful cries of hunger and deprivation, then he'd roll around on his back with his feet in the air, then rub up against the closet where his food was kept, then stare mournfully at his empty bowl. Finally he would jump up on the counter, stare directly into my face with his big, blue, crossed eyes, and let out a series of pitiable squeaks and yelps. At this point I almost always broke down and put a little extra food in his dish, which he would gobble up gratefully, purring all the while and gazing up appreciatively at me from his bowl.

Instead of admitting my guilt, however, I offered up the alternative theory that perhaps Blanche had somehow learned to open the closet door all by himself, and he was sneaking out some cat-food snacks while we were out of the house. Geneen was not amused, and the ensuing discussion quickly deteriorated beyond the bounds of all civil discourse.

Finally, however, I confessed. I promised I would be a more responsible cat parent and would no longer be suckered by Blanche's hangdog (or, rather, hangcat) looks. As soon as Geneen and I had made up, I remembered the magic envelope. So I said, "Hey, do you remember that envelope for solving arguments, from our wedding? Let's take a look in there and see what it says."

Geneen gave me an astonished look and said, "We can't look in the envelope *now.*"

"Why not?"

"Because we're already finished with our argument. Those letters in the envelope are for when you're in the *middle* of an argument!"

I had to admit that she was right. But I desperately wanted to look in the envelope. My curiosity was getting the best of me. A truly demented thought crossed my mind for a fraction of a second—I could pretend to start up another big argument right at that moment, just so I could get the chance to look in the envelope. But I refrained, and domestic tranquillity prevailed. From that moment on, however, we never forgot about the envelope again. Here are some of the ideas it contained.

"Part one, stop whatever you are arguing about," wrote Ritch. "You must each immediately switch sides and argue from the other's position for at least five minutes. Part two, hug each other. Part three, go back to the original fight, if you can."

Sarah took this idea one step further. "Keep up your fighting," she advised, "except from now on you have to sing your words, like you were in an opera!"

Next, a message from an anonymous wedding guest: "Chill out. You can invoke the brachy-cardiac response (slowing down your heart rate) by immersing your face in a large pan of ice-cold water. Sharing one large pan together might also help calm things down."

Stanley wrote a message to my wife on one side of the paper: "This is a personal message for your eyes only. Remember all the times when you've been wrong before? You're probably wrong again. Make up with him now, before it's too late." The power of this injunction was somewhat diluted, however, when compared with the note on the reverse side, addressed to me: "This is a personal message for your eyes only. Remember all the times when you've been wrong before? You're probably wrong again. Make up with her now, before it's too late."

Peter's message said, "Stop talking, and look deeply into

each other's eyes for one full minute. Look at that beautiful soul staring right back at you. After a minute, give each other a great big wet kiss. Do it right now, like you really mean it. Then, if you want to go back to fighting, go right ahead, be my guest. But don't you have something a lot better to do with your lips at this very moment than to start a fight?"

Shelley contributed a suggestion that's certain to end any argument in a hurry: "Quit what you're doing and draw faces on each other's butts with lipstick. Good luck!"

Turn Fights into Frolics — Part III: Let Go of Being Right

The greatest barrier to resolving differences between ourselves and other people is our need to always be right. Throughout the years I have learned that being right is highly overrated. I'm not suggesting that it's great fun to be wrong, but being right isn't everything it's cracked up to be. Furthermore, when we're focused on being right, we're not very likely to engender a life of laughter and play. Being right is serious stuff, and many of us just don't know how to let go of it—even when it's standing in the way of our happiness. We are left with the empty satisfaction of being right and ruining an evening—or a good relationship.

The problem is, most people believe that our interactions with others are a zero-sum game: if you win, then I have to lose. If you're right, then I must be wrong. So we tenaciously defend our position—because it feels so bad, so humiliating, so threatening to our self-esteem to be wrong.

Several years ago I observed the most incredible example of this. I was taking a friend out to celebrate her fortieth birthday, and we invited another couple along. We chose a reasonably nice restaurant that specialized in exotic pastas. First we ordered a bottle of wine, and then we ordered our meals.

As soon as the food arrived things started going wrong. My meal arrived with a long blond hair (which I had not ordered) smartly intertwined with my spaghetti. I politely informed our waiter that there was a hair on my plate. He took my plate back to the kitchen and brought me another order. (Have you ever wondered why it takes them twenty minutes to prepare your meal the first time and only two minutes the second time around?) Anyway, my second plate arrived without the Clairol look, and all was well—for a few minutes. My friend was most of the way through her meal when she noticed a mushroom on her plate that was literally caked with the mulch in which the mushroom was grown. We're talking mushroom stem deep in manure, and on her birthday to boot!

She did exactly what any reasonable diner would do. She called the waiter over and said, "Will you take this back to the cook and ask him if *he* would eat it?"

The waiter said, "Yes, ma'am," picked up her plate, and disappeared into the kitchen.

I don't have to tell you what we expected in this situation, do I? The waiter would return, perhaps with the manager at his side, both of them apologizing profusely. Then they would provide a brand-spanking-new plate of hair-free, manure-free, free-free pasta, and tell the birthday girl that her meal is on the house.

Fat chance. The waiter returned, set the same plate of pasta, with the same turd-festooned mushroom, in front of my friend and said, "Yes, the cook said he would eat that. No problem at all." All four of us responded with a few moments of stunned silence. However, my friend Joan took control of the situation. "Wait just a minute!" she said. "This woman has been served a mushroom surrounded with the manure the mushroom was grown in! I can't believe you would have the nerve to bring that back out here!"

By this time we were beginning to cause a minor commotion, and the manager came over and asked if anything was wrong. Joan assured him that something was. She said to the manager, "This woman has been served a mushroom that is still surrounded by the fertilizer it was grown in, not once but twice!" Now the profuse apologies, right? Wrong again.

The manager very politely said, "That's impossible," and proceeded to give a detailed account of the restaurant's superior mushroom-cleaning system, a multiple-sterilization process that would make Julia Child blush.

At this point I decided that I, somewhat skilled in the art of logic, should enter the fray. "Excuse me just a minute. Do your cooks and other kitchen helpers wear hair nets?" I asked innocently, setting him up for my deft logical move.

"Of course they do," he replied haughtily.

"Well, it looks like even the best systems sometimes do break down, then," I informed him triumphantly. And I proceeded to tell him about the blond noggin noodle that had taken up residence in my first plate of spaghetti.

He dismissed my efforts at an argumentative analogy with a curt "That's not the same thing."

In retrospect I realize that I played an important role in escalating our dining debacle at that point by delivering a piercing blow to his self-esteem. I simply said, "Oh, really? Thank you, you're dismissed."

Then Joan applied what she thought would be the coup de grâce by picking up her napkin, reaching across the table, and saying, "We'll settle this," as she captured the mushroom in question inside her napkin. "I'm sending this mushroom to a friend of mine down at Texas A&M," she told the startled manager. "He will analyze it for me and send the results to the health department. We'll see if they approve of you feeding crap to people on their birthday!"

The manager looked aghast and screamed, "You've contaminated that specimen with your napkin!"

Tom, Joan's husband, said loudly, "Enough is enough already. Let's just pay the check and get out of here."

The manager responded, "Oh, no, I'm taking care of the check for you!" So we argued over that one for a little while. Finally we agreed to let him handle the check, and we got up to leave the restaurant, still arguing about the specimen Joan had tucked inside her purse. It was extremely embarrassing to us to have this wild man escorting us out of the restaurant arguing with us about a mushroom. As we reached the door Joan delivered a final left hook to his ego, "Look, mister, I know everything about growing mushrooms, and this mushroom has crap around it."

Believe it or not, he wasn't even fazed. He actually followed us out of the door and began walking down the street with us, continuing the argument. Undaunted, Joan delivered what we thought would be the *final* final blow. She reached for the stars. No way he was going to top her in this argument. She looked him square in the eye and said, "Look, mister, you can't tell me anything about mushrooms that I don't already know. I used to work on a mushroom farm!"

What followed was perhaps the greatest case of not being able to let go of being right that I have ever heard in my life. The restaurant manager was not going to allow Joan to know more about mushrooms than he did. He stammered, stuttered, and finally got it out: "Well . . . well . . . well, *I am a mushroom!*"

"What?" I said. "You *are* a mushroom?" I doubled over with

laughter. Were there not numerous witnesses, I would have doubted my own ears.

At first, I was laughing at him. Then I laughed at all of us. None of us had been willing to let go of being right. None of us could exchange being right for resolving our dispute.

The manager's behavior, of course, is an extreme and outrageous example of something that many of us do more subtly all the time. We have to be "right" all the time. We pretend to be something we are not. We suffer from false pride. We have difficulty acknowledging our limitations, our lack of knowledge, and our shortcomings. The most tragic consequence is that this attitude costs us dearly in the long run. We could suffer so much less, play so much more, and laugh so much more easily if we could just let go of being right.

There is an old Yiddish story about a rabbi who is asked to resolve a dispute between two neighbors. The first neighbor passionately pleads his case, and the rabbi instantly pronounces his verdict: "You're right!"

"But rabbi," protests the second neighbor. "You haven't even heard my side of the story yet!" And he proceeds to tell his version of the events.

"Yes, I see," comments the rabbi. "It's clear that you're right, too."

"But wait a minute, rabbi," protests an outraged onlooker. "They can't both be right."

"Yes," says the rabbi, nodding sagely. "And you're right, too!"

Once we break away from the straitjacket of a zero-sum existence, we begin to diminish the power that being right has over our lives. We no longer feel a jolt to our self-esteem every time someone disagrees with us. We can see that the world is made up of different points of view, and just because I am right, you are not necessarily wrong.

One of my teachers, Zen master Thich Nhat Hanh, tells his students that we could help ourselves greatly if we posted in our house a sign that we would see on a regular basis: ARE YOU SURE? When we allow the humility that an honest answer to this question demands to inform our lives, then it is much easier to let go of being right. Then we can turn our energies to a much more productive goal—resolving our differences. Very quickly our experiences will teach us that it is much more life-enhancing to be in a successful relationship than it is to hold on to always being right.

Learn
to Laugh at
Yourself

Just for a moment now, if you can stand it, think about your life in junior high or high school. While a few of us had very serious problems to face, most of us were tormenting ourselves about going out on dates, covering up pimples, and deciding what clothes to wear. When you looked back at yourself from the perspective of ten years later, you probably said, "I can't believe all the psychic agony I put myself through over those meaningless problems! What could I have been thinking of!"

Yet while they were happening, those problems didn't seem meaningless at all. Now take a moment to think about the really important problems you are facing in your life at this very moment. Ten years from now you will probably look back at your life today and say, "I cannot believe all that psychic energy I wasted over those simple problems!" (That is, if you can even remember ten years from now that all these things were once problems for you.)

The truth is that we always do the best we can do at any given moment, and at the same time we are continually growing stronger, wiser, and more powerful. No matter how serious the problems facing you may appear to be at the time, there can never be any advantage to taking *yourself* seriously. Every morning upon awakening, do your best to remember that the human condition is a laughable one. Remind yourself that with even the best of intentions there is a good chance you will unintentionally make a fool of yourself that day. Then give yourself the gift of one of the greatest and most liberating pleasures in the world: a huge belly laugh at your own expense.

When we laugh with a friend over a story he tells at his own expense, our heart opens to him. We feel that we are truly human together; our shared laughter at the human experience bonds us. But why should we treat ourselves any less lovingly than we treat our friends? Why not share a laugh with yourself at your own expense? When you learn to take yourself lightly, you open your heart toward your own self. It is when you are at your most serious, when you are feeling the most full of your own importance, that you know the cosmic pratfall must be lurking nearby.

It is very difficult to laugh at yourself when you become puffed up with your own importance. And one sure way to become puffed up about your own importance is to believe that you are somehow special because of how much you know or what you have accomplished. I long ago learned that if I am going to make a habit of reading my press clippings, I had first better develop a sense of humor about myself. In what I thought was going to be the first big break in my career, I was once invited to be the opening speaker at a national conference that was covered by all the major media. I was flushed with excitement after *People* magazine ran my picture and called me "the Master of Playfulness." Later that day I ran into an old friend. "Hey, I was just reading about you in *Time* magazine!" he said.

Thinking that he must mean *People*, I said, "Yeah, wasn't it great?"

"Was it?" he asked dubiously, as he pulled out a copy of *Time* from his briefcase and slid it across the table to me. This article included no photo of me. In fact, the reporter needed only nine words to dismiss my entire presentation. "The day's events began with a short, bouncy loudmouth," he wrote. Hey, cancel my subscription!

Whenever I begin to think that I am really knowledgeable and clever, invariably life grabs me by the lapel and says, "Listen up, fool!" When I'm really lucky, life is pretty subtle and just gives me a gentle nudge. This happens quite frequently, of course, whenever I am in the public eye, and I start to think that all the attention actually means something about who I am. It happened most recently when I started to walk from the stage after giving a breakfast speech to a group of 250 people.

As soon as I was done with my speech, the audience jumped to its feet and gave me a thunderous ovation! I was pleased, of course, and just as my thoughts began to turn to my own cleverness and excellent speaking skills, I looked down and noticed my mismatched shoes.

One was brown, the other was black. In the predawn darkness, in an attempt to get dressed without turning on the light and waking my wife, I obviously had found what felt like a familiar pair of shoes. But in the light of day, it was clear that I had been sadly mistaken.

I thought of telling them the old joke, "I have another pair just like this one back at home." But it was too late at this point for any kind of damage control. During the hour of my talk, I had intentionally walked out from behind the podium, thinking I could make a better connection with the audience that way. But all the time I had been prancing about the stage, I had just been providing them with an ongoing fashion show of how a true dork would get dressed in the morning.

Even as I bathed in the glory of this standing ovation, life was whispering to me, "Lighten up, big shot!" You have to admit it's pretty hard to take yourself seriously when you can't even match your own shoes. I even began to think that the audience was really standing up to get a better look at my feet! When you start having thoughts like that, then laughing at yourself comes very easily.

Of course, as a teacher, I am in the public eye almost every day, whenever I step in front of one of my classes. Being a teacher is excellent training for learning to laugh at yourself. When one is cast in the role, with eager students hanging on your every word, it's fairly easy to start to believe that you are actually pretty clever. But whether in your work life or in other situations, whenever you start to believe that, you are just a short step away from taking yourself too seriously. I discovered the truth of this principle several years ago when I had the good fortune to teach philosophy to a group of American students in Athens.

Americans traveling abroad seem to expect everyone to speak English. So, in an effort to be a good role model for my students, I set myself the goal of learning ten new Greek words a day. Every morning I picked out several useful words and practiced them, then I attempted to use them that day in conversations with our Greek bus driver, shopkeepers, waiters, and tour guides.

As it happened, this particular class had twenty-five students, twenty-two of whom were women. It was not uncommon, therefore, for me to end up going out for dinner in the evening after classes with seven or eight of the young women. On one such occasion, my determination to use Greek proved to be my undoing. I often use pepper on my food, but I rarely add salt. It seemed that restaurants in Athens always put salt on the table but not pepper. So that day I had learned the Greek word for "pepper."

After our dinner of soup (SOO-pa), salad (sa-LA-ta), and string beans (fa-so-LA-kya) arrived (we ate a lot of soup, salad, and string beans on that trip, because I knew the Greek words for those foods), I decided to show off my expanded vocabulary. I asked the waiter to please bring me some pepper; "Pee-PAR-ee pa-ra-ka-LO," I said. The waiter seemed shocked, and he looked at me as though I had slapped him in the face. I was sure I had the right word, so I tried again, with the oft-cited American-abroad habit of speaking *louder* when we're not understood: "PEE-PAR-EE, PEE-PAR-EE, PA-RA-KA-LO!"

This time the waiter took two full steps backward. He surveyed the table of young women with a rather embarrassed look on his face. Customers at the surrounding tables began to look my way. But I'm clever, right? I'm a college professor, right? So, I didn't panic. I simply reached over and picked up the salt shaker in an attempt to use supplemental forms of communication and once more shouted, "Pee-PAR-ee, pee-PAR-ee, pa-ra-ka-LO." A huge smile of relief and understanding came over the waiter's face. He said, "Oh, pee-PEAR-ee!" and rushed away to get the pepper. I thought to myself, "Pee-PAR-ee or pee-PEAR-ee, what's the big difference? What's this guy's problem?"

The waiter returned with the pepper, then hung around the table for quite some time, shooting meaningful glances in my direction, until I realized he wanted to talk to me privately. I waited until the students were all engaged in conversations, then I unobtrusively slid my chair back from the table. The waiter leaned down and quietly said in heavily accented but excellent English, "Sir, when you use the Greek language you must be very careful. A moment ago you used a Greek slang word. What you actually said was 'Bring me a penis, please!' "

So much for the articulate, clever professor being a role model for his students. I could just imagine what the Greek customers in the restaurant must have been thinking. It was on that day that I truly came to realize that regardless of how clever I am or think I am, I am still very laughable.

In the final analysis we are all very laughable, and no matter what the situation—on the job, at home, with our family, even alone—we can remember to laugh at ourselves. In situations like these life is whispering to us, "Hey, aren't you ridiculous!" If we will just open our ears and listen to life, we'll find it more difficult to take ourselves too seriously and very easy to laugh at ourselves.

Remember to Play Under Pressure

A much maligned practice, but one that has nonetheless produced powerful results for many people, is that of using affirmations. An affirmation is a phrase that you repeat over and over in an attempt to produce a positive result in your life. The idea is that the repeated affirmation speaks directly to your subconscious, the part of your mind that can help shape your behavior but that your everyday conscious mind has no awareness of and no control over.

In times of stress and pressure, we often do the opposite of using affirmations to produce positive results: we often repeat "negations" to ourselves. Do you ever notice yourself saying things like, "I'm so stupid! How could I have done that?" or dozens of other equally negative comments? Obviously, in difficult times it would be more useful to have an affirmation to repeat, one that would remind us to treat life as a game.

This approach sounds simple enough. But if it were, we'd all be living more upbeat, stress-free, playful lives, because all of us have already repeated, hundreds of times, the perfect affirmation for learning to laugh and play with life. The problem is that neither our conscious nor unconscious mind has properly understood the true meaning of this affirmation, so we have been unable to unleash its power to shape our lives for the better.

I am referring to the affirmation that begins, "Row, row, row your boat." We've known it and repeated it since we were schoolchildren. And yet, one look around you will show you that this powerful affirmation has had very little positive impact on our culture. Ours is not yet a culture filled with laughter and play. But that can change; with knowledge comes power. Let us examine this affirmation line by line.

Row, row, row your boat. These words tell us that happiness in life is not just handed to us—we must be active participants in creating it. Each of us has our own particular work to do in the world. And by doing that work, whatever it may be, we can find satisfaction, meaning, pleasure, and joy.

Wherever you are in this moment, happiness is available to you, if you just do what your particular situation in life calls for. When you find yourself in a boat, for example, you should row it. And you don't just row once or twice—you need to be persistent. You row, row, row your boat, over and over again.

It doesn't matter that your job may ask you to repeat the same motion, or the same activity, over and over again; this is not a case of "been there, done that," because you haven't ever really been in this very moment before. You've been somewhere very similar, sure, just a moment ago—but you haven't been *here* before. Pay attention to this unique moment. How is it different from the moment just before? How is it unique? How can you make it fresh for yourself?

If you can pay sufficient attention to the present moment,

then nothing is ever boring, nothing is repetitive, nothing grows old. Everything is fresh and new, every moment can give us joy: the third stroke of the oar can be just as special as the first one. It is these simple, everyday pleasures that define our lives and our work and give us our everyday moments of joy.

Gently down the stream. This verse reminds us that we can live our lives gently, without resistance or upset, enjoying the pleasures and lessons that lie around every bend in the stream. All we really need to do is to remember to ride the boat in the direction that it's already going. Of course, sometimes when we are rowing, we will have to mobilize our energy, exert our will, overcome the rocks in our path. But even in these difficult times, our work lives do not have to be constant struggle; they can, rather, be full of ease and purpose, with a clear vision of where we are headed.

When we begin to feel that there is somewhere we ought to be other than where we already are, that things are not moving fast enough in our careers, that there is something else that we need to be doing, then we create upset in our lives. We begin to row madly upstream, leaving worry, turmoil, and dissatisfaction in our wake, splashing everyone around us and creating difficulties left and right.

Once we begin to accept, instead, that where we are right now is exactly where we need to be, that there is no need to panic, that change will happen in its own time, and that there is a surfeit of love, joy, challenge, and satisfaction awaiting us in every moment, right here, right now, then we can truly ride gently down the stream of life.

Merrily, merrily, merrily, merrily. Well, that about says it all: take time to stop and celebrate the everyday joy of being alive. And don't just celebrate it once—do it over and over again.

Take every possible opportunity to rejoice in your life. As I write these words in the first rays of early-morning sunlight, after a freezing night spent shivering under the covers in a rustic country lodge, I look around and ask myself, is there actually anything to be merry about in this miserably cold moment? And of course, there is. The snowcapped mountains are peering spectacularly out from beyond the clouds covering the nearby hills. I hear the sound of the fire warming the hot-water heater for our morning showers. And there is a little, gray, underfed cat snuggling up close to me, trying to keep warm.

And then, all at once, there is the great pleasure of shared company as my hiking companions stumble bleary-eyed into the main lodge and join me in huddling by the fire. One by one they voice the same lament about last night's icy sleeping conditions. Each one attempts to top the others in his description of his suffering.

I sense that they are in no mood to hear my deep thoughts about "merrily, merrily, merrily, merrily," so instead I join in the conversation and share my own experience of refrigerated living. We all share a little half-smile, a look that says, "Ain't it awful, but at least we're in this together." On the outside, we are shivering and moaning, but on the inside, I suspect we are all feeling very merry indeed to be reunited.

Life is but a dream. Notice the verse does not say, "Life is but a nightmare." A nightmare is what your life feels like when you continually row upstream, when you focus on problems instead of opportunities, when you insist on being somewhere other than where you actually are.

But if you do your work, if you ride the stream, if you stop and celebrate your successes along the way, then your life can truly be a dream. And what are the characteristics of a dream? A sense of power, of connection with all things, of joy and liberation. You are not bounded by conventional restrictions of time and space—you can fly through the air, you can speak with the dead. You can do whatever you want to do with your life.

When you begin to sing, "Row, row, row your boat" to yourself once again as an adult, you will find that the tune is quite catchy, and you may have a hard time getting it out of your head. That's fine, because once you understand its true meaning, you will find that it can be quite soothing to repeat it.

The next time you are stopped at a red light, for example, just begin to sing the song softly to yourself under your breath. Notice the pressure that you put yourself under while driving, pressure you may not even have been aware of. Notice the tension in your body as you are seated behind the wheel. Notice your impatience with having to wait at the light, and your anxiety that stopping at the light might cause you to be late for your appointment.

Remind yourself that it is okay to be stopped at the red light, that this is as good a place as any other to be right now. Even though you would rather be speeding along to your ultimate destination, if you reflect on that feeling for a bit, you might change your mind. Zen master Thich Nhat Hanh frequently pointed out to me that for all of us our ultimate destination is the graveyard. So perhaps we shouldn't be in such a hurry to get to the next place without fully living the moment we are in right now. Even your time waiting at the red light can be wonderful. It can be a moment of relaxation, a time to practice being in the present moment. You can actually begin to look forward to red lights, because now they provide time to gather yourself together, to center yourself, to remind yourself to play under pressure.

Notice how different you begin to feel inside your body, how much more relaxed and at ease you have become. And then, when the light finally turns green, you can drive your car confidently ahead, secure in the knowledge that you are now traveling

Gently down the stream,
Merrily, merrily, merrily, merrily,
Life is but a dream.

Dance,
Don't Wrestle

After a glorious picnic at Bachman Lake, my friend Lou Ann and I were driving back home when her car broke down. We were about five blocks from her apartment, and I had just moved to Dallas the week before and didn't know my way around. I started to panic. My head was buzzing as my mind began racing: "*I don't know who to call. Is there a mechanic around here we can trust? Is there a decent garage nearby? Is my AAA card even good in this state?*"

Lou Ann took one look at my hysterical expression and said to me, "Don't worry about it, I'll take care of it tomorrow." Then she pushed me out of the car, locked the doors, reached into the trunk, and pulled out a huge boom box. She pushed a button on the stereo, and an old Teddy Pendergrass song came thundering out, "GET UP, GET DOWN, GET FUNKY, GET LOOSE!" And she started dancing off down the street.

This response to the situation had not occurred to me. I stood flat-footed on the sidewalk, amazed, as the distance between us steadily increased. The music was calling out to me, and Lou Ann gave me a beckoning wave of encouragement. She was obviously not going to turn back for me, and she certainly didn't seem to be concerned about her car. So in the end I had no option except to go dancing off after her.

The possibility of dancing with life's problems is always present for us, if only we know how to listen for the music. Yet too often we find ourselves wrestling with our problems instead of dancing with them. From a distance, dancing and wrestling can, in fact, look very much alike: you see two people with their arms locked around each other, moving in a circle. It's sometimes hard to tell, just by looking, which is which. But dancing and wrestling with your problems are certainly not the same thing. The difference, of course, is that when you wrestle with a problem you resist it, you fight against it, you try to impose your sense of order on the chaos of the world. When you dance with a problem, however, you flow with it, you stay open to all possible solutions, you search for a harmonious resolution. And, amazingly enough, you try to enjoy yourself in the process.

Aikido, one of the Eastern martial arts, is based upon this simple but profound philosophical principle. Rather than overcoming your opponent by meeting his aggression with your own aggressive force, you flow with his aggression to resolve the conflict. True, the opponent is sometimes hurt in the process; however, it is because his own aggression has done him in. By dancing with his aggressive behavior instead of wrestling with it, you are merely rechanneling his attack in a way that brings positive results for you.

Fortunately, this aikido-like approach is also available to us in the nonphysical confrontations we all must cope with on a regular basis—at work, at home, and in every other area of life.

For example, several years ago I was accosted by one of my neighbors, a person I had always known only as "the woman in the green dress." Even though she had been my neighbor for six years, I had never really met her or learned her name. And in all those times that I saw her, save one, she was always wearing what appeared to be the same green dress. (One day I saw her in an ill-fitting brown dress. The reason for her short-lived flirtation with sartorial diversity remains a mystery to this day.)

I had, in fact, made several attempts to befriend this woman over the years. When I first moved into the neighborhood I would wave at her as I went off on my daily run, but to no avail. She would turn up her nose and look away. I never had any idea what I might have done to offend her, but she obviously wanted nothing to do with me. Then one day I was backing my car out of my driveway, and after more than six years of silence, who should be shouting at me from across the street but the woman in the green dress. She came striding across the street full-tilt, a look of anger in her eyes, holding a stick she habitually carried—I had always supposed—as a defense against rabid dogs or hostile neighbors.

I stopped the car and rolled down the window, surprised and perplexed at this change in her behavior. The woman in the green dress was obviously about to unload on me.

And unload she certainly did! Before she even reached my car, she started chewing me out about my dog. She told me my dog was turning over her garbage can and spreading trash all over the yard. She told me I had better keep my dog tied up or she was going to call the pound. She pointed an accusing finger at the dog that was currently standing innocently in my front yard.

My guilt about her accusations was lessened considerably by the fact that at that time I didn't even have a dog. The dog she was pointing to was my next-door neighbor's sweet old hound, Alice. Alice visited my house only occasionally to get into the garbage and to poop in my yard, which she was doing quite gleefully as the woman in the green dress continued her tirade. I tried several times to get a word in edgewise, without success. She would hear none of my excuses. She was going to make sure I got the message loud and clear.

I began to get very irritated. However, just before I started to scream back at the woman in the green dress and give her a piece of my mind, I remembered to ask myself, "Do I really want to start wrestling with this woman? How can I flow with her, instead of fighting against her?" And in that moment, I realized how I could turn the battle into a dance. Without a word, I threw open the car door, jumped out of the car, and looked straight at her. I shrieked, "You know, you're right! *Let's kill that dog!*" And I then proceeded to chase the befuddled Alice around the yard.

The woman in the green dress appeared to be even more startled by my reaction than I had been when she first waddled across the street in my direction. She started screaming after me, *"No! No, wait! We don't have to go that far! We don't have to kill the dog!"* She must have thought I was completely insane, because she backed quickly away from me and retreated to the other side of the street. To my knowledge she has never crossed that boundary again.

Whenever I am confronted with difficult situations and resist my first impulse to strike back, to be hostile or aggressive, things go better for me and for those around me. If I take a few moments to relax and think about how to dance rather than wrestle with the situation, then I am nearly always rewarded with a solution that is ultimately more creative, more peaceful, less stressful, and much more productive.

It's unfortunate that there must sometimes be barriers among human beings; however, it is inevitable that we will occasionally make a few enemies. We are all going to come in contact with sour, angry people. We are undoubtedly going to be confronted with negative situations and difficulties in work and in our personal lives. Even in those trying times, however, we can find ways to be playful and to view those situations as an invitation to dance.

Learn the Wisdom of Water

One of the hardest lessons I've learned, one that I have to constantly relearn, is how to *relax*. Whenever people ask me how they can learn to be more relaxed, I usually suggest that they take a couple of hours and go sit beside a creek, a brook, or a river and see if they can learn the wisdom of the water. If you're having difficulty relaxing, you might want to try it too. Water doesn't struggle, it just flows. When it's confronted with an obstacle like a rock, water doesn't get upset or aggressive, it just relaxes and flows around the rock. If you could hang around long enough, you would notice that eventually the water has its way and it wears the rock down.

Eastern philosophers have a saying, "You can't catch running water in a bucket." The idea, of course, is that once you capture the water in the bucket, you will have standing water. If you want to have running water, then you must be willing to let go. This is one of the most difficult life lessons for many of us—that is, sometimes in order to have something you want, you must be willing to let it go.

When I was a boy my mother would come into my room and say, "All right! You've got to try to go to sleep!" Have you ever been successful when you've *tried* to go to sleep? It won't happen. Rather, you must be willing to flow like water, to let go of all the trying, and then sleep will wash over you. By using water as a metaphor for living, we begin to develop an attitude that I call natural relaxedness. Water is just quite naturally relaxed about things. When we develop this attitude we create a relaxed life for ourselves, and we tend to help others relax as well.

Of course, there are times to hold on, just as there are times to let go. Wisdom, I believe, is knowing which action is called for in a particular situation. Experience has taught me that when I am confronted with negativity, hostility, anger, and aggression, it is definitely a time for letting go. It is a time to flow with the wisdom of water. Now, I'm not suggesting that whenever we confront hostility or aggression on the part of other people we should just let ourselves go with the flow, allow ourselves to be run over and become passive wimps. I am merely saying that we can relax and take life less seriously if we quit struggling so much and let our first thought be about the wisdom in water. So many times in our lives we could bring about more positive, laughter-producing, relaxing results if we first ask ourselves, "How would water handle this?"

You may be thinking that every time you confront an obstacle at work or in other critical situations, you won't have the time, availability, or the resources to go sit calmly by a stream. As the Spanish philosopher Ortega y Gassett once wrote, "Life is fired at us point-blank." To most of us it seems that life is not only fired at us from close range, but that it is coming at us from a rapid-fire, automatic weapon. Most of our problems won't wait while we go sit by a river to figure things out. When a walk to a stream is out of the question, however, we can at least take a walk across the office, open the refrigerator, and stare at a bottle of Evian. We can take a few deep breaths and ask ourselves, "What would water do?"

I remember asking myself this question when I realized that my daughter would be unable to enter first grade because her birthday was two months too late. Rachel's birthday is in November, and the schools in Texas require that a child reach her sixth birthday by September 1 if she is to begin first grade that year. I had many friends in the field of education assuring me that Rachel was mature beyond her years (she was already reading, writing, and using a vocabulary that far exceeded that of the average six-year-old), and I was convinced that it was the right time for her to begin first grade. I was also convinced by my friends in public-school education that there was no way I could wade through all the red tape and bureaucratic roadblocks involved in getting Rachel admitted as an exception to the rule. So I told myself that my only hope of success was to act like water and flow around the system.

I didn't have to think too long before I came to the conclusion that if I wasn't able to change the school system, then I was going to have to change Rachel's birthday. Since it was July, I had very little trouble convincing Rachel that it would be really neat to change her birthday from November 10 to August 10. So the only real problem was finding a way to change her birth certificate to reflect father and daughter's wise decision. After carefully studying Rachel's Dallas County birth certificate, I reluctantly decided that forgery was out of the question. The only solution was for Rachel to have a new county of birth. To be on the safe side I decided that a new state would even be better. Next I decided that I had to choose a state where it was likely that Rachel could have been delivered at home, without the assistance of a doctor, which would explain the fact that she didn't have a birth certificate.

The rest was easy. I wrote a letter to Montgomery, Alabama, explaining that my daughter was born on August 10, 1973, in the backwoods of Montgomery County, on the Coosa River. I went on to explain that she was delivered at home by a midwife, and that I had failed to register her birth at the time. Within a month I was in possession of an official birth certificate for my daughter, which allowed her to enter first grade in Dallas. She has done quite well in school ever since.

As any parent might guess, when October rolled around I had no trouble convincing my daughter that it wasn't such a good idea to change her birthday to August after all. We decided that although we didn't need to tell the school officials about it, it would be really neat to change her birthday back to November again; she could have two birthdays that year.

When we learn to relax around our problems, and flow like water, we often find that the solution can be effortless. When the ancient Chinese philosophers first suggested that we use water as a metaphor for how we should live in our daily lives, moving Rachel's birthday around was probably not the kind of thing they had in mind. In fact, now, some twenty years later, it might not even be what I would have in mind. As a lifelong student of ethics, I know clearly that Kant would see it as a violation of the Categorical Imperative. And Hobbes would find it at odds with the Social Contract. But then again, Bentham and the Utilitarians would surely spring to my defense by acknowledging that what I did produced the greatest good for the greatest number of those affected.

So, even the great moral theorists might not agree fully on the morality of my actions. I doubt, however, that the Montgomery County officials would ever find my actions legally amusing. That being the case, perhaps the more appropriate question we should ask ourselves when confronted with obstacles or difficulties is not only, "How would water handle this?" but also, "How would water handle this . . . legally!"

Make
Your Ordeals
Benevolent

Some years ago I was very surprised to learn from a colleague of mine, Gary Verett, that he and I share a goal in life that is near and dear to my heart—living a carefree, hassle-free, ordeal-free existence. For the more than fifteen years in which Gary and I had been colleagues, I couldn't recall even one other time that we had ever agreed about anything. In fact, I often thought anyone who wanted to find out what kind of person I am could simply get to know Gary and picture his opposite.

The following example may give you some idea about our differences. Gary is a psychology professor. When he wants to demonstrate anal-compulsive personality traits, he takes the class on a field trip to his own office. There they find everything carefully planned and placed, right down to the last paper clip. My office, on the other hand, is the Bermuda Triangle of offices. Over the years, many things have gone into my office, never to be seen or heard from again.

I was so astounded to hear Gary mention his goal of having an ordeal-free life that I took him aside to inquire further into the matter. When I told him that I too had this goal, he was amazed. "What?" he exclaimed. "You go through life literally begging for hassles! Your life is an ordeal just waiting to happen. For heaven's sake, half the time you're lucky if you can even get your socks to match!"

I responded casually that it was no small feat to get my socks to match every day, as it seemed like one of them got lost every time I did the laundry. But just because one of my favorite socks was temporarily lost, that didn't mean I shouldn't wear the other one in the meantime, did it? But Gary was undaunted. He proceeded to explain to me his very rational and orderly method for keeping up with his socks. (In fact, the next time we saw each other he generously presented me with a package of sock matchers, little plastic rings one can use to hold a pair of dirty socks together in the wash. Needless to say, I had never heard of sock matchers before; it is one of the most astonishing gifts I have ever received.)

Somewhere in the middle of this conversation with Gary I had a profound insight. Although he and I were in full agreement about the goal of having a hassle-free existence, our approaches were diametrically opposed. Essentially, I believe that Gary is trying to arrange the world in such a way that it will not be an ordeal for him. I, on the other hand, am trying to arrange myself so that the world with all its ordeals will not be a problem for me.

Gary has a system for virtually everything in his life, and then another system to back up the first one. He goes so far in trying to make sure that the world doesn't present him with ordeals for which he is not prepared that he even has a backup

Weed Whacker! If his first line of defense against weeds fails, then he can always turn to his reserve Weed Whacker without missing a moment of useful activity.

Now, I'm not suggesting that Gary's approach is necessarily wrong. Certainly, it's good to be prepared. If we could just fix the world so that we wouldn't have any ordeals, that would be a great thing. However, I believe that no matter how much time, energy, creativity, and skill we invest in trying to fix the world (and, of course, everyone in it) to make it ordeal-free, we can't get it all done. We are still going to be confronted with crises.

Sigmund Freud once wrote, "Life is a problem for everyone." I think this is one of his conclusions with which even his most ardent detractors must agree. The poet Rainer Maria Rilke said much the same thing in a somewhat more poetic way: "Life has a rhythm of sorrow for all of us." No matter how much we try to control exterior factors in our lives, and no matter how many backup systems we have in place, life will present us with hassles, problems, and sorrows. At times life itself is an ordeal.

If we accept that our lives will sometimes present us with ordeals, then our challenge is to learn to make those ordeals as benevolent as they can be. That is, we must temper our ordeals—as much as possible—by kindliness, pleasure, generosity, laughter, play, joy, prosperity, and goodwill. We can accept that life has a rhythm of sorrow, but we need not accept the idea that we are powerless to change that sorrowful state.

I was introduced to the idea of a "benevolent ordeal" a few years ago as a result of a conversation my wife had with our good friend Marge Takai. For many years I had given my wife the same answer to her question about what I wanted for my birthday: "Oh, nothing, there's not really anything I want." That year, however, I had not given her the standard answer. This time to her annual question I gave an unequivocal reply: "I want a golden retriever puppy!"

After waiting all these years for a specific answer, she was not happy with the one she got. She was, to say the least, not enthusiastic about the idea of a puppy running around the house. But Marge had the solution for her. "Just give him a benevolent ordeal, and he'll forget all about the idea of getting a puppy."

"A benevolent ordeal?"

"Yes," Marge explained. "Just give him some hoops to jump through as a precondition to getting the puppy, and believe me, the puppy thing will blow over in no time. But you make it fun for him, so even though it's a hassle, he still can have a good time with it." So, they brainstormed and came up with the appropriate benevolent ordeal. My wife came home and calmly announced that if I could get one thousand signatures on a petition in favor of the puppy and present it to her a week before my birthday, then the puppy would be mine.

Years later my wife said that she knew she was in trouble when I went to my computer and typed out the following petition:

We the undersigned give our full support to the concept
    that the petitioner should have a golden retriever
    puppy for his birthday.
Given that he has, like most persons of his age,
Suffered numerous hardships in his life, and that even so
    he has managed to avoid getting
Mired in cosmic bitterness, and further that he has never
    really had a puppy to call his own,
We feel that his request for a puppy is reasonable and just.
In short, we the undersigned believe that he deserves a
    puppy.

I made several copies of the petition and then rushed up to the entrance of the grocery store, where people often stood with petitions. As Marge had predicted, I was having fun. I would say to shoppers, "Will you sign my petition?" They would usually say, "What's it about?" I'd say, "I'm trying to get a puppy." Usually, they would read the petition and laugh. Often they would rush off to find their friends to come back and sign, too. However, at the end of an hour I had only forty-one signatures.

I knew that a thousand signatures was going to be a real ordeal. So, I did what any puppy-desperate man would do. I faxed a copy of the petition to several of my close friends and to two of my children who were college students and asked them to help. I also had the opportunity in the next week to give two different speeches to large audiences, so I took the petition along. My audiences were wildly enthusiastic in their support of the project. And my allies across the country reported similar successes. My son Kevin even set up a Puppy Petition booth in the cafeteria of his college. The tide was turning!

One friend who sent me a petition with more than three hundred signatures reported that it gave him great joy to walk up to perfect strangers and ask if they would be willing to sign a petition so that his friend could get a puppy. "Sure," they would say. "How old is your little friend?" He reported that he got some very strange looks when he said, "Forty-seven."

I collected more than five thousand signatures in just over three weeks. As the signed petitions began pouring in from all over the country, my wife even got caught up in the fun. When she took one of the petitions with her to work, I knew the puppy would be mine.

Even more important, however, was that what had originally been a real problem for my wife (and what she had transformed into a benevolent ordeal for me) became a source of joy not only to both of us but to thousands of other people. When we approach an ordeal with an attitude of lighthearted kindness, playfulness, and fun, we can change a potentially negative situation into a wonderful experience for everyone involved.

Life will invariably give us ordeals to face. Our choice is either to get mired in the negativity of these problem situations or to remember that even an ordeal can sometimes be benevolent.

Be Happy
When Things
Change

Two thousand people were staring in my direction. I was looking at them, but they weren't looking at me. Not yet, anyway. I was waiting to give a talk to the incoming freshmen at Baylor University, who were spread out in front of me on the floor of a huge gymnasium. The dean of students was the speaker before me, and I was half listening to his speech about the long Baylor tradition of academic excellence and half rehearsing my own speech. I was sinking deeper and deeper into a reverie about what I would say when all of a sudden the dean got my complete attention. With no warning, he shot his right arm out in front of him, formed his fingers into a claw shape, and then vibrated his hand rapidly from left to right, all the while loudly chanting, "Aaaahhhhhh . . ."

An electricity gripped the room. Instantly, all two thousand students responded in kind, their hands turned into claws, a guttural yell filling the gymnasium: "Aaaahhh-hhh . . ."

The dean looked left, looked right, and, apparently satisfied that the crowd had worked itself to an appropriately feverish pitch, waved his clawed hand up and down and yelled out, *"Sic 'em, Bears!"*

In one voice, the students echoed his call: "SIC 'EM, BEARS!" and the gymnasium erupted into a pulsing, cheering celebration.

Amazed, I turned to the person seated next to me and asked him, "What in the world was that all about?"

"Oh," he replied offhandedly, "our football team is the Baylor Bears. That's just our football chant. We do it at all the games."

"Oh, okay, fine." I nodded knowingly.

Finally it was my turn. About five minutes into my talk, one of the students suddenly jumped to his feet and spontaneously started the big "Aaaahhhhhh . . ." The rest of the student body instantly joined in. Having seen it all before, I happily abandoned my speech and joined in as well, turning my hand into a claw, and chanting, "Aaaahhhhhh . . ." along with the best of them.

This went on for what seemed like a long time. A very long time. "All right," I thought to myself impatiently, "let's get on with it already." But the students seemed content to let the big "Aaaahhhhhh" stretch on interminably.

Finally it dawned on me that the students were waiting for me to lead them in the end of the chant. I rapidly moved my clawed hand up and down, as two thousand voices joined me in shouting out, "SIC 'EM, BEARS!" and the place exploded in pandemonium.

It was an exhilarating feeling, as if the entire audience was engaged in an experience of improvisational play together. It was so much fun that I tried it again. And again. And every time I inserted "SIC 'EM, BEARS!" into my speech, the audience erupted into wild cheers. It certainly wasn't the speech I had planned to present, but in the end it was one of the most fun talks I ever gave. Shouting "SIC 'EM, BEARS!" was one of those unexpected pleasures whose memory brought a smile to my face for quite some time afterward.

In fact, for the next several weeks, whenever anyone asked me, "What's new?" I invariably launched into recounting my adventure with the Baylor Bears. I found myself joyfully telling the story to anyone who would listen. On one of those occasions I was having lunch with Stuart Brown, an expert on playfulness in animals. Stuart had promised to share some of his research with me during lunch, and he soon topped my story with a bear story of his own. His story helped me understand that the reason my experience with the Baylor Bears felt so important to me was because it was a story about learning to play with change.

"The end seemed very near for Hudson, a Canadian Eskimo dog," recounted Stuart. "A thousand-pound polar bear was lumbering toward the tethered dog and about forty other dogs, the prized possessions of Brian Ladoon, a hunter and trapper. It was mid-November 1992. Ice had not yet formed on Hudson Bay east of Churchill, Manitoba, and the open water prevented the bears from hunting their favorite prey, seals. So this bear had been virtually fasting for four months. Surely one of the dogs was destined to become a meal.

"The bear closed in. Did Hudson howl in terror and try to flee? On the contrary. He wagged his tail, grinned, and actually bowed to the bear, as if in invitation. The bear responded with enthusiastic body language and nonaggressive facial signals. These two normally antagonistic species were speaking the same language: 'Let's play!'

"Soon the romp was on. For several minutes the dog and the bear wrestled and cavorted. Once the bear completely wrapped himself around the dog like a friendly white cloud. The bear and the dog then embraced, as if in sheer abandon. Overheated by his smaller playmate's shenanigans, the bear lay down and called for a time-out.

"Every evening for more than a week the bear returned to play with the dog. Finally the ice formed, and he set off for his winter habitat." At this point Stuart triumphantly displayed a *National Geographic* article he had written about the dog and bear encounter, complete with photographs of the astonishing event.

"This is unbelievable!" I exclaimed, looking through the collection of photographs. "But I don't get it. If the bear was hungry, why didn't it eat the dog? Why would the bear want to play with it instead?"

"Why do bears play?" responded Stuart with a laugh. "That's a great question, and it's exactly the question I asked Bob Fagen, who knows all about bears and play. One time we were watching some black bears frolic together, and after some hesitation, without looking up, Bob said to me, 'Because it's fun.'

" 'No, Bob, I mean from a scientific point of view, why do they play?'

" 'Why do they play? Why do birds sing, why do people dance—for the aesthetic pleasure of it.'

" 'Bob,' I said, 'you have a degree from MIT, a Ph.D. in ethology, an in-depth knowledge of bears. You're a student of evolution—you've written the definitive work on all mammals and birds at play; I know you have other opinions about this. Why do these bears play?'

"With some further hesitation, he finally answered thoughtfully, 'In a world continuously presenting unique challenges and ambiguity, play prepares them for an evolving planet.' "

In other words, the act of play prepares the bears to adapt to the constantly changing environment that every living being confronts every day. And in the same way that play can prepare bears for a life of constant change, so too can it prepare us humans.

During improvisational play, we experiment with a new set of skills that can help us cope with times of change. Playing is a way of trying on new behaviors, of adding something different to our repertoire of responses. When we "play" with a problem, we approach it differently, creatively, we have fun with it. Because we don't take it seriously, we don't act rigidly, and therefore we are free to discover new and unusual solutions. We look at things from a fresh point of view, as though we are seeing them for the first time. We give ourselves permission to experiment, to move outside our usual patterns of behavior.

And so, when it then comes time to act "for real," we don't have to do what's always been done—instead, we can do whatever is called for, whatever is appropriate to the moment. We can improvise a creative solution, just as we do during improvisational play.

One of the most stressful changes that can happen in anyone's life is having to move our home or our place of business. We get attached to our physical location, and when we are forced to change it, to leave our home base, to clear out years of accumulated junk, we get upset. Even if we ourselves initiate the change, even if we are dying to move, it can still be a difficult experience.

When Gaia Bookstore in Berkeley, California, decided to expand into the space next door, the staff decided to have some fun with the remodeling process. Before the expanded store was to be repainted, they invited their customers to join them in a repainting job of their own. Employees, customers, and even the UPS man when he came to make a delivery were handed paint and paintbrushes and were asked to leave their mark on the walls. People wrote letters and poems, signed their names, and drew pictures, knowing that this burst of creative expression would soon be painted over.

The employees realized that since the walls were to be torn down and rebuilt all around them, they had a unique opportunity to leave a message in the walls for future generations. As a final work of conceptual art, they readied a time capsule, to be buried deep within the walls of their remodeled building. Inside their time capsule they placed books, pens, the bookstore's calendar of upcoming events, money (for good luck), samples of merchandise sold by the store, and handwritten notes. "It turned some of the stress of remodeling into a fun and a thought-provoking event for all of us," remembers store owner Patrice Wynne.

There is an old saying that goes The only difference between people who are alive and people who are dead is that dead people do the same thing every day. In that same way, people who are afraid of change also want to do the same thing every day. And in that way, they might as well be dead to their lives, and to the opportunity to play with the game of life. A constantly changing world calls for constantly changing responses, both in our business lives and in our personal lives. And a playful attitude toward life can help us to cope with those changes—and to actually enjoy them as they happen.

The worst thing a fan can say about a sporting event is that it was boring.

"How was the game?"

"It was soooooo boring. Nothing happened."

We like our games filled with action, unpredictability, change. Every inning should be unique, every quarter should be different from the last one, and every game should be something special.

That's how the game of life should be, too. Every day should bring something new for us to experience, and every moment should be a chance to play with life a little differently from the moment before. Yet for some reason, many people are afraid of change in their lives. Instead of embracing change, we try to hold on to our experience, to make it predictable, the same as it always has been. Whatever feels familiar also feels safe to us, so any kind of change can feel threatening. But the more we can learn to play with change, the easier it becomes to welcome it into our lives.

It is in times of change that we can feel the most fully alive. If we don't want to be left behind, if we want to live in the moment, in today's world instead of yesterday's, then we need to welcome change, not hide from it. We need to ride with it, not run from it. We need to use our playful skills to help us embrace change, instead of being afraid of it. We can learn to approach change with arms wide open, because a time of change is an invitation to come out and play.

SIC 'EM, BEARS!

III

Learning to Laugh and Play with Life

Surround Yourself with People Who Like to Laugh and Play

It is one thing to read about a life of laughter and play, and it is another thing entirely to experience it. The best way to make it happen is to surround yourself with people who like to laugh and play, people who can support you and inspire you in your quest for a more playful lifestyle.

I like to think of a group like this as a "play community"—people who gather together to support the unfurling of one another's playful nature. Play is their common language and their common purpose. Buddhist practice has a wonderful term for this: a *sangha*. A *sangha* is a group of people who gather with a common intention, usually to do a spiritual practice or perform a service together. The idea of a *sangha* is that it is easier to do your practice when you are supported by like-minded individuals who are practicing along with you. And since it takes practice to lead a life of laughter and play, it makes sense to gather a *sangha*, a play community, around you—playmates who can share in the joy of your practice.

I inadvertently stumbled on my first (and ultimately longest-lasting) play community one summer when my friend Marty decided to throw himself the ultimate birthday party. To celebrate in style, he invited twenty of his friends to accompany him on a river-rafting trip on the Rogue River in southern Oregon.

The Rogue is categorized as a Wild and Scenic river, which means that the landscape is spectacular, the rapids are treacherous, and the number of visitors is strictly limited as part of the federal protection program. As we floated down the river we passed salmon spawning upstream and deer staring out at us from the edge of the forest. Families of ducks swam alongside us. One day we even saw a huge black bear, fishing for salmon from the riverbank.

We rode swirling, white-water rapids in big inflatable rafts, and we jumped off the rafts to ride them in inner tubes, screaming and terrified but in control of our own destinies. The river guides called out to us about the safest ways to navigate the tricky waters, but we invariably capsized in our tubes, and hung on for dear life as rocks, waves, and whirlpools rushed by us.

In the long stretches of calm water we formed huge chains of tubers (or "spuds," as we called ourselves), linked together and floating downstream, talking animatedly, getting to know one another better.

It was an ecstatic experience.

The next year when Marty proposed a reunion birthday party, I eagerly signed up. The second year was, if anything, even better than the first. At the end of the four-day trip, my friends Amo and Ritch ran up to me, bubbling over with excitement. "We're going to take a vow to do this trip every year for the rest of our lives!" they passionately exclaimed. "Don't even think about it! Let's take the pledge together!" And we did.

Now, twenty years later, there is a long-standing core group of five men and five women who have taken this pledge, to float together on the Rogue River every year for the rest of our lives. Each year another thirteen people join up with this core group to form a floating community of twenty-three tubers and four river guides. The ten vow-takers have flown to the Rogue from as far away as Hawaii and Australia in order to honor their yearly pledge. And at the end of each trip, we gather together and recommit: "Every year for the rest of our lives! Every year for the rest of our lives!"

Of course, over twenty years there have been scores of other people who have come to the end of the trip and have gratefully taken the opposite vow: "Never again as long as I live! Never again as long as I live!"

Many of the veteran tubers I see only once a year, and yet it feels like we're family whenever we come together again, same time, next year. When we enter the magical world of the river trip, we call one another by the nicknames we've developed over the years. I hardly know their real names anymore; to me they're Phoenix, Otter, Spirit, and Laughing Man. Most of them, in turn, only know me as Igor. (It's a long story—don't ask!)

There have been a few years when I haven't felt like going on the trip, or when I was so overwhelmed with work that I told myself I couldn't afford to take the time off. At those times I have cursed my damned vow, then reluctantly dragged myself up to the river, knowing that I certainly wouldn't be doing so if I hadn't given my word. And yet every one of those times, floating serenely in my tube in the midst of incredible scenic beauty, forced into the present moment by the sound of approaching white water around the next bend, I have said to myself, "What could I have been thinking of, to ever think of missing this trip? How could I have forgotten how much I love it here? There is no place on earth I would rather be than right here, right now!"

Taking the vow has protected me from my own worst workaholic tendencies and has carved out a huge portal in my life for laughter and play to enter at the same time every year. Surrounding myself with people who were crazy enough to invent such a vow, yet serious enough about their sense of a play community to honor that vow for more than twenty years, has given me the support to bring this week of wild joy into my life, year after year. It is a gift to myself that I can always count on, a gift that will undoubtedly continue . . . every year for the rest of our lives!

39

Give Your Friends a Year of Fun

Consider the people you think of as your friends. Do they like to laugh and play? If not, then you might want to consider finding some new friends. If you were to make a list of the people in your life who could form your play community, which of them would be on that list? Once your list reaches at least twelve people, think about inviting them all to a party and enacting the strategy for building a play community that was developed by my friend Mahalia Pugatch.

Mahalia gathered many of her friends together for a party at her house and brought out a calendar for the upcoming year. She talked about the way we had all begun to lose touch with one another, as we had all become more successful and responsible in our careers. "It's as if our lives are all about work now, and not about fun or friendship or community anymore!" she said indignantly. So Mahalia proposed that we remedy that with "a year of having fun."

She spread the calendar out on the floor and asked for one volunteer for each month of the year. Each person would be responsible for organizing one fun event for the community, so by the end of the evening we would have planned one get-together for every month. "Call me in a week and let me know the date of your event and what you have planned," Mahalia told the volunteers. "Then I'll send out a one-page calendar of events to everybody here—something that you can hang on your refrigerator door so you can't forget about it."

That year we had potluck dinners and dance parties; we went bowling, hiking, and Sufi dancing together. We even had Colander Head Night, where each person had to decorate a colander and then wear it as a hat all night in order to gain admission to the party.

Ready to form your play community? The first step is to surround yourself with people who like to laugh and play. Then organize some volunteers, and get ready for a year of having fun.

40

Stay in Touch
with Your Friends

One of the principal difficulties of having a job that re-
quires frequent out-of-town business trips is that it can
play havoc with your family life. But fortunately, modern
technology has made it possible to stay in constant communication with your family and friends, wherever you
are. Even when you travel far from home, you never have
to be without their support. Whenever Amo Tarnoff, one
of the Playfair trainers, goes away from home on an ex-
tended business trip, he records a videotaped message
that he leaves behind for his two young sons to play every
night before they go to sleep, so they can feel their
father's presence at home with them. And the kids record
messages to their dad on his voice mail several times a
week. Audiotape, videotape, voice mail, E-mail, telephone, videophone, overnight mail—the list of the ways
modern technology can help you keep in touch goes on.

Yet impressive as all these technological advances may be, technology, as Sigmund Freud pointed out nearly seventy years ago, is a double-edged sword: technological advances do not necessarily make our lives any happier. In his book *Civilization and Its Discontents,* Freud explained that the invention of the telephone made it possible for him to hear the voice of his child who lived hundreds of miles away, and it enabled him to know instantaneously that a friend has arrived safely at the end of a long voyage. But does that mean, asks Freud, that technological advances like the telephone provide us with "a positive pleasure, an unequivocal gain in happiness?" Not necessarily, because at the same time, "if there were no railway to make light of distances, my child would never have left home, and I should not need the telephone to hear his voice. If there were no vessels crossing the ocean, my friend would never have embarked on his voyage, and I should not need the telephone to relieve my anxiety about him."

In the many decades that have passed since Freud wrote these words, technology has become more deeply embedded in our way of life. Nowadays we think nothing of picking up the phone to talk to relatives across the country, of sending E-mail messages to friends across the planet, or of jumping onto a jet plane on the spur of the moment.

In Freud's day, traveling to another continent was a significant and time-consuming venture, not something that the average person undertook lightly. Long-distance travel took considerable planning and foresight. Calendars were consulted well in advance of the departure date, and large blocks of time had to be cleared to make the long and arduous trip. So it is likely that if Freud were to take a vacation trip to, say, Hawaii, he would have noticed well in advance of the day that he was to set sail that he had a conflicting social event on his calendar.

Whether because I am a product of my era or for some obscure psychological reasons (reasons Freud certainly would be more qualified to comment on than I would), I found myself in a different situation when, the week before I was to depart for a romantic vacation in Hawaii with my wife, I realized that I was scheduled to travel on the same day as the 49ers-Cowboys playoff game.

Now, I don't want you to assume that I'm some sort of football fanatic—far from it. Watching football is a community event for me, a gathering of friends at the home of whichever one of us can afford to buy the biggest television set. Watching a football game by myself is a dreary, boring affair, something I would rarely do. But after all, this was the 49ers and the Cowboys. This was the Playoffs.

I was quite distraught over this impending conflict in my schedule. Changing the flight at this late date so that I could watch the game with my friends was completely out of the question. But to miss the game altogether, to be left out of this preeminent cultural event in the life of my community, to have to look on blankly whenever my friends reminisced about the Big Game . . . that was a fate too bleak to contemplate.

So I confided the dilemma to Geneen and threw myself on her mercy. "Honey," I said, "there are two solutions that I can think of. One is that when we get off the plane in Honolulu, we can go to a bar in the airport and watch the game; and then after the game is over we can catch the next flight out to the Big Island. Or else maybe I can get one of the guys to videotape the game and overnight it to me at the hotel."

To say that my wife is not a big football fan is a gross understatement. She thinks of football as a violent and idiotic pastime, and she flees from the room, muttering abusive comments under her breath, anytime a game comes on the television. I could just imagine the response my proposal was likely to elicit. "Perhaps you have overlooked option number three," she would say. "That you and I are going away together on a romantic vacation. That our idea of a romantic getaway is supposed to be just the two of us alone on a tropical beach together, with no distractions at all. Just the two of us. Alone. With no work to do. No telephones to answer. *And definitely no watching any moronic football games!*"

But instead, she surprised me. She must have realized how much this game meant to me, because with a bemused shrug that clearly communicated that I was a pitiful creature who owed her a big favor, she said, "Okay, then have them send you the video."

The resort where we were staying truly was romantic, designed to replicate the feeling of an ancient Hawaiian village. Each couple had their own *hale*, a Hawaiian bungalow with a thatched roof. As advertised, there were no telephones and no televisions in the rooms, just complete privacy. In fact, on the entire property there was only one television and one video player, which was used for showing movies of the Hawaiian volcano to a handful of entertainment-starved tourists every Tuesday night. This equipment was stored in the room that overlooked the barbecue pit for the luau, and it was to that room that I eagerly made my way once my precious overnight package had arrived from the mainland.

My friends back home had truly outdone themselves this time. They had sent not only a videotape of the game but also an audiotape of themselves watching the game, so that I could experience the game along with them. I slipped the audiotape into my Walkman, put on my headphones, started up the video, and sat back to enjoy the experience.

I suppose it was the incongruous sight of someone watching a football game and laughing hysterically at the same time that attracted the assistant manager of the resort over to my side for a closer look. What had me laughing were the comments that my friends directed to me on the audiotape: "Can you believe that bonehead play?" "Did you see that pathetic pass?" "I wish somebody would just shoot me and put me out of my misery!" They included me in the conversation, as though I were actually in the room with them.

As soon as I saw the assistant manager approaching me, I pulled off the headphones and called out to him, "It's the 49ers-Cowboys game from last Sunday. *Don't tell me who won!*"

He nodded, then asked me about the headphones. I told him about my friends' commentary, and I gave him the headphones. After a few moments he broke into an unbelieving grin. "Your friends sent you this tape of themselves? That's so great!"

Since I couldn't fast-forward through the commercials (in order to keep the audiotape properly synched with the videotape they had to keep running simultaneously), there was plenty of opportunity for the assistant manager and me to talk during the breaks in the action. He asked me how I was enjoying my stay, and I told him that we had vacationed at the resort many times before, including our honeymoon. We always stayed in our favorite secluded *hale* on the pond, but there was one small problem this time. There was a construction crew working on the thatched roof of the *hale* next door, and the resulting noise was making it difficult for us to relax.

He thanked me for my frankness and promised to see what he could do to remedy the situation. After watching a bit more of the game, he left me to return to his official duties. I stayed and watched until the end of the game, suspended in my time warp. As soon as I put the headphones back on, I entered a separate reality; I was instantly able to turn back the clock two days and experience Sunday afternoon at home with my friends on a Tuesday afternoon in Hawaii.

When the game ended, I returned to my room to discover

that my new pal the assistant manager had upgraded my wife and me to an exclusive beachfront *hale,* which normally would have cost us an extra two hundred dollars a night.

Now, I'm not saying that this extravagant upgrade would never have happened if I hadn't had my electronic community sent to me in Hawaii. But I do know that the assistant manager got a big kick out of putting on the headphones and traveling back through time with me and my friends.

It never hurts to surround yourself with people who like to laugh and play, even if they're only on tape. The next time you're traveling away from home on business, bring along some audio or video recordings of your loved ones. And the next time a friend is traveling, pull out the camcorder, gather some friends, and send a surprise video message overnight to his hotel. It's the next best thing to being there.

41

Live *in* the Moment
(Not *for* the Moment)

My friend Mahalia Pugatch has a master's degree in dance, has learned to whirl like a dervish for hours on end, teaches classes in sacred religious dances of the world, and likes nothing better than to stay up late, exhausting her partners on the dance floor for half the night. The bumper sticker on her car proudly proclaims, I'D RATHER BE DANCING!

One day I noticed that her bumper sticker was gone; a few shreds of torn paper hanging from the bumper were all that remained in its former place of honor. It was clear that the bumper sticker had been removed on purpose. "What's the matter, don't you like dancing anymore?" I jokingly asked her, nodding toward the rear of her car.

"Oh, no, that's not it at all," she replied earnestly. "Of course I still love dancing, in fact I'm going out dancing tonight. But that's not the point. Last week I was driving along and I suddenly realized that my bumper sticker was saying to the world that I'd rather be doing something other than what I'm doing right now. What does that say about my life—that I can't be happy doing whatever I'm doing at this moment? That I'm waiting around for a better life to arrive someday? Forget it! So I pulled over to the side of the road, and I ripped the damned thing right off my car!"

Mahalia makes a very good point about one of the ways that we keep ourselves from making the most of our lives. Instead of living in the present, we spend far too much time waiting for some magical moment that we imagine will occur in the future. And when we aren't being hijacked into some idealized vision of the future, then we are likely to be caught reliving some moment in the past. And what's worse, the moments that we often choose to relive are difficult memories that make us feel negative, anxious, and filled with stress.

This way of relating to life has had a strong influence on our popular culture. We can see this very clearly in the titles of two hit songs from my teen years. The Beatles sang "I Want to Hold Your Hand," an excellent example of anticipating pleasure in the future instead of finding it in the present. And then the Rolling Stones followed with "(I Can't Get No) Satisfaction." So it seems in the world of pop culture that even if sometime in the future we are finally able to hold hands, we are still somehow left dissatisfied.

"I can't get no satisfaction" is an expression that captures the emptiness that so many people feel about their daily lives at work, at home, and even at what they call play. Why are so many of us unsatisfied? Why is it that so few of us can live a life that is filled with moment after moment of laughter and play?

The advertising industry is well aware of this chronic illness in our society. Notice that some of the most frequently used words in advertisements are *better, more, new,* and *improved.* The subtle but very clear message, of course, is that we need something different, something more, something better than this moment. The present is simply not good enough.

Compare this view of life with the story about Native American warriors who, before going into a battle, were reported to say, "Today would be a good day to die." I have always understood this as an expression of the fullness of their lives at that very moment. The idea is not so much that on any particular day it is good to die but more that if I should die right now, then my life would have been good enough, because I have learned to live fully in this moment.

One of the best mantras we can use to enhance our daily lives is "This is good enough." If we could just remember, several times a day—whatever we are doing—to take a deep breath and repeat to ourselves, "This moment is good enough," perhaps we could cure some of the chronic dissatisfaction that so often haunts us.

My oldest uncle taught me many lessons about living the good life. He was not "successful" by many people's standards. He never made much money. He never owned a nice car or his own house. He didn't have a prestigious job. Yet, I remember many times when we were together enjoying a peaceful walk in the park, or looking at the first stars of the evening from our swing on the front porch, or sitting by a slow-moving stream: he would take a deep breath and say with great irony, "I wonder what the poor people are doing right now."

Even as a child I understood that he was communicating to me the wisdom of living in the moment. He was telling me that by paying attention to the incredible richness with which the natural world continually surrounds us, we were very rich in that moment, no matter what our material wealth. Contrariwise, no matter how much "wealth" or "success" we think we have, the quality of our life will be very poor if we do not know how to be here now. In short, there is no better get-rich-quick scheme than that of learning to live in the moment.

However, we should not confuse living *in* the moment with living *for* the moment. A philosophy first expressed in ancient Greece by Aristippus, and which has gathered many contemporary adherents, promotes the idea that we should simply live for the moment; that is, now is all we have, so go for it all right now. Their reasoning goes something like this: life can only be experienced one moment at a time; the only pleasure we can truly experience is our own pleasure; physical pleasure is the most intense of all pleasures; the future is uncertain at best—so let's indulge our desires, to our heart's content.

Advertisers have tried to capture the essence of this philosophy, which is basically egoistic and hedonistic, with such phrases as, "Reach for the gusto," "Go for the gold," "Life is short, play hard." Unfortunately, when we pursue that "ultimate high" that is supposed to come from living for the moment, we find that when the high passes we are left dealing with the inevitable "low" that follows. The most fundamental flaw in the "Eat, drink, and be merry, for tomorrow you may die" philosophy is that often tomorrow comes and we don't die. Instead, we are left wandering around in a daze, looking for relief from the intense suffering that goes with overeating, too much drinking, and not enough sleep.

Rather than saying, "Today would be a good day to die," we find ourselves saying, "I wish I were dead." Living *in* the moment allows us to discover that life is good enough, whereas living *for* the moment leaves us saying, "Is this all there is?"

That wise old uncle of mine—when we were fishing and having no luck—was also fond of saying, "Pull up your line, son, we're going to a worser spot!" In his brilliant but subtle way he was always reinforcing the same idea: value the moment in which you are alive right now, because it can be wonderful. Don't spend your time waiting for an unknown future to arrive, because who knows what the next moment will actually bring?

42

Sing More,
Complain Less

One thing that keeps us from the laughter, play, and joy that is readily available to us is the habit of complaining. We complain when things change. We complain if they don't. We complain on the job. We complain at home. We complain about the government. We complain about the lack of government. We complain about the weather. We complain about people who complain. For many of us, a good deal of everyday life is spent complaining.

If we want to live the good and happy life, there are some habits we need to avoid and others we need to acquire. In my estimation, complaining is in the category of the former, while singing is of the latter. To me it seems rather obvious that we should spend more time singing and less time complaining. When we complain, it is usually because we feel powerless, fearful, or depressed about our lives. Naturally, when we have these feelings we find it much more difficult to laugh and play. Also, when we realize that most of our complaining comes from our fearfulness, depression, and feelings of not having enough control, then we can also see that complaining is not really an authentic solution to our problems.

I believe that much, if not most, of our fear and depression comes from a feeling of being limited and stuck—in other words, feeling that we are without options. A genuine solution to our feelings of limitation and constriction comes through our ability to be creative, to imagine other possibilities. Through imagination and creativity, we can really produce change.

Stay with me on this one, now. Let's assume that creativity is the cure for feelings of limitation. Singing is, of course, just one of many forms of creative expression, while complaining is not. Singing is a sign of being free, while complaining is a sign of being stuck.

Since the time of the ancient Greeks, philosophers have pointed out that it is possible to take control of the way we view the world. And yet, throughout the ages, most people have chosen to see themselves as victims of circumstance instead. They find it easier to complain about life than to change the way they live. The advice of the philosopher Epictetus still rings true in the present day: "[People] are disturbed not by things, but the views which they take of things. When, therefore, we are hindered or disturbed, or grieved, let us never impute it to others, but to ourselves—that is, to our own views. It is the action of an uninstructed person to reproach others for his own misfortunes; of one entering upon instruction, to reproach himself; and one perfectly instructed to reproach neither others or himself."

Given that you have a choice to view things positively or negatively, there is no reason to choose to live in ways that are detrimental to your health and well-being. One of the most interesting things about this habit of complaining is that none of us really likes being around people who complain all the time. Yet we do little to reduce our own complaining. So, if you are looking for a surefire way to change your life for the better, then here it is: sing more, complain less.

Then again, some of you may say what I hear so often when I suggest to people that they do more singing: "I can't sing!" I can certainly understand this; I've said it myself. Then one day my friend Peter Alsop, a talented singer and composer, taught me a wonderful life lesson. In response to my comment "I can't sing," Peter simply said, "Oh, yes, you can sing, it's just that you have a bad voice!" Of course, he was right. We all can sing. Some of us just have less wonderful voices than others.

If you're not convinced that singing more and complaining less is a good idea, ask yourself the following questions: in what way does complaining benefit us?

"Well," you might say, "unless I complain I can't bring about change."

That's fair. So, we can give the stamp of approval to all complaining that is directly related to bringing about positive changes. For example, pointing out to our supervisor that there is not enough laughter and play in our work environment *and* proposing solutions to the problem seems like healthy and wholesome complaining.

On the other hand, most complaining is not directed toward positive change and, therefore, is rather unproductive. Clearly, this latter kind of complaining does not serve us well. In addition to making us negative people who seem to be hopelessly mired in the reliving of negative situations, it wastes valuable time that we could be using for any number of life-enhancing activities, not the least of which are laughing and playing.

While I know of no scientific evidence to prove that singing contributes to one's health and well-being, anecdotal evidence abounds. If you like, do your own research. Ask your friends if they like being around people who complain a lot. Then ask them if they would prefer someone who doesn't complain much but who occasionally breaks into song. Look critically at people who are chronic complainers and compare your perception of their lives with those who are chronic singers. My guess is that your research will confirm my own findings. Singing has few costs and great benefits, whereas complaining has few benefits and enormous costs.

It is true, of course, that for many people life is hard. It is much easier for most of us to find things about which we can complain than to find things that make us feel like singing. One particularly effective technique for turning our attention away from the negative toward the more positive aspects of life was taught to me by a Zen master. He suggested that when we are feeling pretty bad about our current state—that is, when we have had one of *those* days, then we should ask ourselves the question, "What's not wrong?" When we don't feel like singing but instead feel like complaining about our lives, then we can focus on what is not wrong in our lives. After all, people are always asking themselves and others, "What's wrong?" Why not shift our attention to what's not wrong? Even when we're not having a bad day, it is still useful to ask ourselves this question. Our internal dialogue might go something like this:

"What's not wrong?"

"Well, I don't have athlete's foot."

"What's not wrong?"

"I still have a steady paycheck."

"What's not wrong?"

"At least my dog still likes me."

"What's not wrong?"

"The photocopy machine isn't broken this week."

"What's not wrong?"

"My senses of sight and smell are working quite well, and there are many wonderful fragrances and sights in my garden."

"What's not wrong?"

"I haven't lost my ability to imagine."

"What's not wrong?"

"I can sing!"

43

Remember
You Are a Human Being,
Not a Computer

Does a warning to remember that you are not a computer seem completely unnecessary to you? After all, how could we forget that we're human?

It is undeniably true, however, that people often fall into the trap of automatic, machinelike living. Rather than living spontaneously and freely, we come to accept the notion that there is a particular way to be a human being. We try to figure out the "right way" to act, think, or feel in a certain situation. We become very uncomfortable when we come into a situation in which we don't know how we are supposed to be.

Not long ago I had a student who couldn't see. I usually spend the first few days of classes getting to know my students and letting them get to know me. On the second day of class this young man said to me in private, "I would like everyone in the class to know that I'm blind."

I told him I thought that everyone had already figured that out, since most students don't come to class with a guide dog.

He laughed and said, "No, I just mean I want to publicly tell everyone that I can't see, and that's all. No one has to act any differently toward me."

When I asked him to explain further, he said, "Well, it's like people get real uncomfortable around me, and I can feel it, and it's just because they don't know how to act. The truth is that I just want people to be who they are and let me be who I am. It just so happens that part of who I am is that I'm blind. Sometimes I feel that when people meet me *all* they can see is that I'm blind. When that happens, they just don't know how to be."

This student was very clearly pointing out one of the problems of automatic living. We become computerlike in our responses to other people, and whenever we confront something unusual or different, the computer shuts down. It's as though we don't have the correct software package for the situation.

Someone once asked the psychologist Erich Fromm whether he thought it would ever be possible to make a computer that is just like a human being. Fromm responded that actually it would be quite easy to do if human beings continue their current pattern of turning themselves into machines. If we start to believe that there is a particular way to be in a situation, then soon all human spontaneity is drained from us and we might as well be machines. Computers are nice things, but they are just that—things. They can be programmed to laugh, play, tell jokes, and respond in all sorts of interesting ways. Yet all these responses are automatic rather than authentic. If we are to live fully, then we must live as authentic spontaneous beings.

Occasionally when I walk around town and someone automatically asks, "How are you?" I stop and ponder the question. Then I give a real answer, and we usually have a good laugh at ourselves, being reminded we are humans rather than computers programmed to say, "Fine!" Or sometimes around holiday time when a salesperson says, "Happy holidays," I respond, "Appropriate remark!" and the same phenomenon takes place.

Some years ago I read that a California legislator had jokingly proposed the death penalty for any salesperson who said, "Have a nice day!" Of course someone can very humanly and sincerely speak those words, but you know as well as I do that most of the time those responses are perfunctory and automatic, devoid of any real feeling.

Once when I was having lunch with my friend Scott Jones, the waitress gave us our check and said, "Have a nice day." Scott replied, "Thanks, but I've already made other plans!" This unexpected remark jolted the three of us into actually paying some attention to one another for a moment. As we laughed together, Scott's little joke gave us a chance to notice that it didn't take much effort to make a genuine connection, and a pleasureful one at that.

Computers can be programmed to laugh and play, but they can't feel the joy and happiness that comes from authentic human play. Thankfully, we can!

44

Take Pleasure in the Little Moments

After I had presented a lecture about fun at work to the National Wellness Conference, I spoke briefly with a few people from the audience who had questions about how to apply these principles to their specific work situations. Just as I had finished talking with the last person in line, I noticed a man walking briskly up the aisle toward me. I looked up to greet him, and the first thing he said was "I want you to know that I have not been waiting around here the whole time just to talk to you like those other people were. My wife and I both enjoyed your talk, but not *that* much!"

"Okay," I offered, attempting to be friendly but wondering apprehensively what was to come next. "So why are you still here, then?"

"Actually, we left as soon as your talk was over," he continued. "And just as we got outside, my wife remembered that she had left her camera under the seat. Now, I want to tell you that usually I would start yelling at her for being so stupid and for making us walk all the way back here, but for some reason I just couldn't do it this time. All I could think of was 'Why choose stress? If life is a game, then this must be part of it! Why get all bent out of shape?' And so we just walked back here together and we got the camera, and it was no big deal, and we both feel fine, and we didn't get upset, and I just wanted you to know that this stuff you're teaching really works."

I felt wonderful about the conversation, because that man had truly grasped the idea that life is a game, and that we really can choose to live our lives as play. It's not just in the big moments that we need to remember this, because life is mostly made up of little moments like this one. If we are going to really have joy and pleasure in our lives, then we are going to have to remember to take pleasure in the little moments.

In order to enjoy the little moments, however, we must first notice them. Paying attention to the little moments is not so easy when we are always busy doing other things. That great philosopher Winnie the Pooh had the idea that we had become a bunch of "Bisy backsons." You know the type—people who are too busy to talk to you right now but say they'll call you back soon. But if too much of our time is spent rushing about doing our busyness, then we will surely miss completely the pleasure of the little moments.

One of the things that a good working dog must master is to sit and stay when necessary—another way we could all benefit from learning to work like a dog. If we want the good, peaceful, playful, joyful life, then sometimes we must learn to be still.

Socrates, Buddha, Moses, and Jesus all taught through their example that we need to take time in our life to be still. When we stop all the rushing and slow down, we are much more likely to experience the pleasure of the little moments, some of the most wonderful experiences in life.

There is a gardenia bush outside the Playfair office, and whenever it is in bloom I make it an everyday ritual to stop and sniff the blossoms on my way in the door. Likewise, whenever the plum trees around our office are fruiting, I take great delight in plucking off a plum whenever I enter or leave the building. My wife has taught me how wonderful it can be when I am spending the day at home to take one freshly cut flower from our garden each morning and put it in a bud vase on my desk. Then, as I go through the day, if I can just remember to stop for a moment to look at the flower, my whole day can be transformed positively in that small moment. I recently put the message "Breathe and smile" on my computer's screen saver. Seeing and heeding this helpful reminder provides me with nourishing breaks in my day. All of us can find ways to create little joyful moments for ourselves in our workday. There is no cost, but the rewards are great.

Many of us, however, are far too focused on the "big moments." We think that there will be such great pleasure in our lives when we get that promotion, or that hefty raise, or get to go on that big vacation. But when we stay focused on only the big moments (which are few and far between), then we miss the major portion of our lives. A friend of mine once pointed out to me that a round of golf takes about four hours, but you spend only about three minutes swinging the club. If you're going to get the most pleasure out of a game of golf, then you've got to learn to enjoy the moments between the swings—the little moments in the game.

Think about some of the great pleasures that take place in life's little moments. There is great pleasure in lying in bed on a very cold morning and curling up your legs—if you take the time to notice. What a joy it is to slice a watermelon on a really hot day—if you take the time to notice.

I once heard a story about a monk who returned to his tent one evening and discovered a thief stealing his meager possessions. As the thief started to make his escape, the monk offered him his robe as well. As the thief ran away, the monk settled himself calmly on the ground, and with a smile of pleasure on his peaceful face he said, "I wish that I could give him this breeze. I wish I could give him this moon."

Like the breeze and the moon, there are joyful, nourishing little things that are constantly available to us, no matter what the external circumstances of our lives—but only if we have first learned to take pleasure in the little moments.

Don't Count
Your Nightmares
Until They Hatch

A fairly popular bumper sticker in the past few years simply states, SHIT HAPPENS. Subsequently I've seen bumper messages that proclaim, in an attempt at bumper-sticker dueling, GOOD STUFF HAPPENS. Now, I believe that those people displaying the second bumper sticker have misunderstood the first bumper sticker; I think "Shit happens" means that things happen, not necessarily that bad things happen.

Nonetheless, in my own wish to reconcile differences, no matter how small, I still considered creating my own bumper sticker, which would read, CAN WE ALL AGREE THAT STUFF HAPPENS, SOME GOOD AND SOME NOT SO GOOD? Or, more subtly: LIFE IS FILLED WITH BOTH FLOWERS AND GARBAGE. I finally gave up on the idea and decided that my bumper was much too small to adequately address a philosophical issue of this importance.

Life confronts us daily with both positive and negative aspects, possibilities, and realities. As a result, we all fantasize about our prospects for the future, and we can imagine either a positive or a negative outcome.

Fantasy can be a very good practice. We must willingly enter the realm of vivid imagination if we want to live a creative and exciting life. Too often, however, we are drawn to negative fantasies. Rather than investigate the question "What's wrong?" or, even better, the question "What's not wrong?" we delve into the world of negative fantasy—"What could possibly go wrong?" Our imagination starts to create one negative scenario after another. As we know from experience, most of our negative fantasies never become reality; but we continue to waste lots of energy on them anyway.

Entertaining negative fantasies not only makes life more difficult to affirm, it can also lead to self-fulfilling prophecies; that is, our belief that something negative will happen can actually play a role in bringing about a negative result. So it is a very good practice to avoid negative fantasies altogether. We can be sure that life will present us with enough negative reality to cope with, without our having to invent any more of it. Life will go much better for us if, rather than fantasizing the negative, we wait until something negative actually happens and then cope with it in the best way we can.

This doesn't mean that good planning, goal setting, and other future-directed activities are senseless. It simply means that imagining all of the negative and awful things that can happen to us isn't a very productive way to live, and it certainly interferes with a life of laughter and play.

This lesson came back to me recently when I received a letter from the Internal Revenue Service. Most of us probably feel that any letter from the IRS that doesn't show a check through the address window is a little ominous. We probably start the negative fantasies before we even open the letter. "Uh-oh, they caught me! I'm going to jail! They're going to take away my house and my youngest child! I'm gonna be bankrupt!"

I must admit that I experienced a slight wave of nausea upon receiving the letter, which was thick and, I could tell, checkless. However, before opening it, I quickly remembered the guiding principle "Don't count your nightmares until they hatch."

The letter nicely informed me that I had incorrectly reported my taxes, and that the IRS would "like to recalculate" my tax obligation. They found that, after their recalculation, I owed an additional $387.00, including penalties and interest. The letter also included a sheet to return within thirty days indicating that I agreed or disagreed with their findings. If I disagreed, then I needed to send appropriate documentation to support my position.

I immediately slipped into a negative fantasy and began to imagine myself, pressed for time, poring through bulging shoe boxes filled with tax records and receipts. After all, how could I agree or disagree without completely redoing my taxes? Horrors! Even worse, the year in question was two years before. I can hardly remember what I spent last week!

Then I remembered again my "No negative fantasies" mantra. I began to think about ways that I could avoid choosing stress and, instead, play with the situation. I quickly jotted down the following handwritten note.

Dear IRS Person,

Thank you for your recent letter. If I was in error in reporting my taxes, then I assure you it was an honest mistake. Your letter asks me to either agree or disagree with your findings; however, I can do neither, because I honestly don't know and don't have the time to find out. I've always let my banker keep up with *my bank balance, so I guess it is a good idea to let the IRS figure my taxes. So, enclosed is a check for $387. You may cash it if you promise to double-check my taxes and make sure I made a mistake. Thanks for your hard work.*

I dropped the letter to the IRS in the mail and practiced letting go of the tension by asking myself, "What's not wrong?" Immediately, I realized that the fact that I had $387 to send to the IRS was a good thing, that it could have been $3,870, and that the suffering I had avoided by taking this approach had saved me hours of poring over tax records. Actually, this alone was probably worth the $387 it had cost me.

Nearly a month later, I received another letter from the IRS. Remembering my successful practice with the last letter, I just breathed and smiled. My smile turned to laughter when I opened the letter. This one thanked me for my recent letter and informed me that the IRS had in fact recalculated my tax obligation, as I had requested. They decided that *they* had made a mistake and *owed me* $115, and that I would be receiving a check within sixty days. They were "sorry for any inconvenience" I might have been caused.

Once again, the lesson of avoiding negative fantasies was powerfully reinforced.

Practice
Having Fun
—— Part I:
What Do You Like
About Yourself?

If you are to live a life of laughter and play, it is not enough just to read about it and think about it—you have to translate it into action, to practice it in your own life every day.

We've all heard the expression "Practice makes perfect." That idea is decidedly false. I have never understood why anyone would think that doing something repeatedly would bring about perfection, especially if one is repeatedly doing it the wrong way. It's like saying that someone who has overcooked thousands of meals has become an "expert" chef.

I think it makes much more sense to say, "Practice makes permanent." In other words, if we practice something enough, it becomes habitual. And if we want to live a good life, one that is meaningful, joyful, and happy, we need lots and lots of practice. We need to try out and rehearse ways of being in the world that will bring about the life skills we want to develop, and we also need to make these ways of walking the earth habitual. That is why these next two chapters contain specific "practices," exercises that can help you develop some of the qualities that can assist you in living a more playful, joyful life.

A previous chapter talked about the importance of remembering that you are a gift. It's not easy to learn to value your inner qualities when our culture places such a heavy value on externals. And when we do think about our internal qualities, we usually focus on the things that are wrong with us, not what's right with us. As a result, your harshest critic on this entire planet is the person seated in your chair right now. Your inner critic berates you in a tone of voice that you would never tolerate from anyone else.

When you take the time to appreciate the things you like about yourself, you take a step closer to silencing that inner critic and to realizing that you actually are a gift. You will need a partner to help you with this practice, so enlist the help of your spouse, lover, or a close friend. Think of yourself as a human being with all of your component parts—your emotional, physical, spiritual, and intellectual sides; yourself as a friend, as a parent, as a child, as a working person.

Have your partner ask you the following question: "What do you like about yourself?" Then respond with the first thing that pops into your head. Then have your partner ask the same question again: "What do you like about yourself?" In fact, that is all your partner is going to say to you over and over again, for a minute and a half. It goes something like this:

Partner: "What do you like about yourself?"
You: "Well, I'm a pretty good conversationalist."
Partner: "That's great! What else do you like about yourself?"

You:	"I'm a really good friend."
Partner:	"Fantastic! What else do you like about yourself?"
You:	"I'm incredibly trustworthy."
Partner:	"Fabulous! What else do you like about yourself?"
You:	"Ahhhh . . . could you please repeat the question?"

Almost everybody blanks out at some time during the course of this practice. All you need to do when that happens is to shoot both your hands over your head in a gesture of triumph and shout out at the top of your lungs: "EVERYTHING!"

Then have your partner ask you the question again. If you still blank out, shout "EVERYTHING!" again. This positive body position usually liberates your mind in a matter of seconds, so pretty soon you're back on a roll:

You:	"I'm a really caring parent!"
Partner:	"Great! What else do you like about yourself?"
You:	"I'm very kind to animals."

You get the idea. Have your partner write down all your answers on a sheet of paper. You might want to carry this piece of paper around with you for a while, to remind yourself of some of the things you value about yourself but that you sometimes forget to notice.

After the ninety seconds have elapsed, take a few minutes to flesh out some of the qualities you've mentioned. Tell your partner how you got to be a person like that—for example, were your parents a positive or a negative role model for you in that regard? What is a concrete example of a time and place in your life where you exhibit this particular quality—does it happen more often in your personal or your professional life?

Then you and your partner reverse roles, with you being the support person and asking the question. Chances are, it will have been such an enjoyable experience the first time around that your partner will leap at this opportunity to extend the intimacy of the moment with you by playing a second round.

47

Practice
Having Fun
Part II:
What Can You Change?

If you want to become more comfortable playing with change in your life, it can be very helpful to first identify three or four simple things that you do regularly and habitually. Not necessarily things that need to be changed but things that you do without much thought, like getting up on the same side of the bed, opening doors with your right hand, or turning your car radio on for the drive to work. You may need to reflect on this for a while, because many of the things we do habitually go unnoticed.

After you have identified these three or four things, change them in a small way for the next week. Get out of bed on the opposite side. Open doors with your left hand. Leave the radio off. As you embrace these small changes, pay attention to your thoughts, feelings, and reactions. See what you can learn about your own ability or inability to play with change. After a week of trying out several simple changes, you may well be ready to play with other, more meaningful changes, changes that will help you live a more vital and playful life. You may be more prepared to embrace the inevitable change that *is* life. To paraphrase the ancient philosopher Heraclitus, the only thing in life that doesn't change is change itself. If change changed, then it wouldn't be change!

Over the past several years, I have been a member of a group that begins each of its meetings with a practice that we call Flowers and Garbage, named after the idea in Chapter 24. This practice gives us the opportunity to check in with one another before we get on with the business of the meeting, and it has been incredibly helpful in establishing a feeling of openness and trust among the group members. We learn about one another's lives in a way that we ordinarily can't do under the pressures of a hectic workday, and we set a relaxed and open tone for our meetings. It gives us a chance to slow down at the start of the meeting, take stock of ourselves, and remember that we actually enjoy working together.

Sharing your flowers and garbage can also give the group participants a sense of ongoing history with one another, as people's lives change over time. One man who reports nothing but garbage, week after week, suddenly has a life in which flowers start to appear. And sometimes, if we remember well enough, we can see that without the garbage of the previous weeks, the flowers would not have been possible. We get to see during our time together that things do not happen in isolation, but that there is a pattern to our lives. We get to see that the only constant in our lives is that things change.

If you'd like to try this practice with your coworkers, invite everyone to pull their chairs into a circle, and give them some instructions like the following:

"Let's each take a few moments to share with the group one thing that's happened in our lives since our last meeting.

This experience is called Flowers and Garbage, because you can share a positive thing (a flower) or a negative thing (some garbage). You can choose either one, it doesn't matter. In fact, don't tell us whether it's flowers or garbage—let us figure it out. Sometimes it's not that easy to tell. It's like that old story:

A man falls out of an airplane.
Fortunately, there is a haystack underneath him.
Unfortunately, there's a pitchfork sticking out of the
haystack.
Fortunately, he misses the pitchfork.
Unfortunately, he misses the haystack.

"So who knows if your story is a fortunate or an unfortunate one? Flowers can turn into garbage, and garbage can turn into flowers."

Don't Repress Your Natural Urge to Play

Why is it that we love to share stories about our playful escapades with all our friends? After we've done something fun, we can't keep it to ourselves. It is often just as much fun to recount these events over and over again as it is to live through them the first time. I believe this is because the urge toward playfulness is deeply rooted in the most primitive pleasure centers of our brain. The impulse to play is one of humanity's oldest treasures.

As I understand it, at the dawn of civilization our species loved nothing more than to play, and that joyful playfulness was the main characteristic that set us apart from the other species. But as is so often the case in life, that which was our greatest joy was also our greatest sorrow.

First, the joy: wherever you looked you could find primitive families hanging around the old cave, frolicking, cavorting, and carrying on playfully, which always resulted in great peals of primitive laughter. As you probably have already discovered in your own life, hearty laughter always brings deep muscle relaxation; many of us have laughed so hard we have fallen off our chairs. So these primitive ancestors of ours would spend much of the time slumped on the ground, gasping for breath from having laughed so hard, the very picture of domestic bliss.

Now for the sorrowful part. At this point some ferocious predator, the likes of which you cannot even imagine in your wildest nightmares, enters the scene. I am talking saber-toothed tigers here. I am talking woolly mammoths with huge tusks. I am talking wolves the size of horses.

Can you imagine how hard it is to pick up a club and defend yourself against an attacking saber-toothed tiger after you've been laughing hysterically for half an hour? Try it sometime with those rubbery, relaxed arms of yours. Believe me, the joke got old very fast. So pretty soon the elders of the community realized that there was something very dangerous in their idyllic, playful lifestyle. You could crack a good joke, and before you stopped laughing half your family would be gone.

So the elders decided that for the protection of the race there would have to be certain rules and regulations drawn up, and civilization as we know it was born. The basic message of these rules and regulations was that adult members of the population had to be ready at all times to defend the community from four-legged assaults, and so they had better stop laughing, smiling, and playing so much. They had better start learning how to be serious and solemn instead. Play became the province of children, and since childhood ended and adulthood began at about ten years old in those days, playfulness soon became a lost art.

I don't mean to imply that these rules did not stand us all in good stead over the intervening millennia. It is likely that we would not be here today to think about these great matters if our forefathers and foremothers had not learned to stop fooling around all the time and take life more seriously. But as with so many of our modern-day cultural guidelines and taboos, we still follow rules and regulations about the appropriateness of adult playfulness that were handed down to us throughout history, even though the times and situations that made those guidelines necessary are no longer operative.

It is no longer true that our lives can be threatened by too much playful behavior. In point of fact, exactly the opposite is true: as recent medical research into the nature of stress clearly shows, our physical well-being is currently being threatened by too much *unplayful* behavior!

In support of my theory that the urge toward playful behavior is one of our most primitive instincts, I offer the evidence of my former career as a high school teacher in the New York City school system. It was during my days as an English teacher that I first discovered that the joy of play can be so strong that it overcomes our cultural conditioning to behave in a mature or "appropriate" manner. This was the case for one of my favorite students, Charlie Barrigan, who was considered a discipline problem by the other teachers because of his uncontrollable urge to have fun in the classroom at all times.

Charlie was half Irish and half Puerto Rican, and he very strongly identified with the Puerto Rican side of his heritage. Unfortunately, this met with disapproval from his Irish father, who absolutely forbade him to dress in the flamboyant Puerto Rican style. So Charlie was forced to dress in two sets of clothes every morning. There was one for his father to see at the breakfast table, a rather conservative, almost preppy-looking outfit. Underneath the preppy clothes, which he peeled off as soon as he got to school, he wore a pair of green checkered pants and a bright red shirt; in his school locker he kept a hat with a flashy ribbon around the brim, to top off the outfit.

Charlie and I hit it off right away in our class. He was full of good cheer, had a quick wit, and laughed at my jokes. I knew he was learning quite a bit in my class, and I didn't see him as a discipline problem. He had one good friend in the class, a Puerto Rican boy named William Rodriguez, whom he loved to torment. As a result of William's fiery temper, they would frequently wind up leaping across their desks to do battle with each other, to the general entertainment of the rest of the class. I was forced, in desperation, to put them on opposite sides of the room and to give Charlie a good talking-to.

The problem was that Charlie knew he could always get a rise out of William simply by mentioning William's mother. So at the most unexpected times, when I would ask the class a perfectly innocent question, Charlie would suddenly shout out, "William's mother!" William, without stopping to think, would instantly leap into action, springing across the classroom and wrestling Charlie to the ground.

Charlie was a tough little fighter, but usually he was so convulsed with laughter at his own wit that he would be defenseless under William's assault.

One morning I was preparing to give this class a vocabulary lecture about words like *quadruped* and *brachiate*. Since I was planning to use the great apes as the framework for my lesson, I realized that I could be asking for trouble. So I took Charlie aside at the beginning of the class and warned him that I really wanted him to lay off William for the next hour. I told him that I knew that it would be very hard for him to not mention William's mother during this particular lesson, but I urged him, for his own sake and for mine, to keep his big mouth shut.

We moved quickly through the chimpanzees, through their abilities as tool-making creatures, through Jane Goodall's observations of chimpanzees in the wild. I glanced over at Charlie, and he gave me a tense smile. We moved on to the gorillas, and talked about how they were truly gentle beasts. The students were surprised to learn that they were vegetarians, and that their fierce King Kong image was an erroneous one. Charlie by now was white as a sheet and trembling. Finally came the moment of truth. I prepared to introduce the orangutans.

"There is one more species of apes in the great ape family," I announced. "Does anyone know what they are called?" I stared directly at Charlie, giving him the moral support he needed to hold himself in check. But the temptation was too much for him. He leaped to his feet and screamed out at the top of his lungs, "WILLIAM'S MOTHER!" I joined William in tackling Charlie and pummeling him to the ground.

I offer this incident as proof of my theory that the urge to play is stronger, more primitive, and more powerful than even the urge for self-preservation. Charlie had learned the lessons of self-preservation that the most powerful agent of our civilized culture, the New York City public school system, had taught him. But when push came to shove, his more deeply rooted instincts to live the playful life proved to be impossible for him to resist.

Yet, if Charlie had curbed his playful instincts, as I had so foolishly urged him to do, I wouldn't have this pleasurable memory. For it is often our playful times that are the most profoundly memorable for us. Memories of playful interactions give us the most pleasure in the retelling, time after time. Frequently we remember them for many years after we have forgotten all the other everyday events that surrounded them. We do ourselves and our companions a great service when we refuse to repress our natural urge to play.

Create
Some Playful
Memories

A prevalent philosophical theory of humor says that humor is a response to restraint. This, of course, explains why people often laugh at really inappropriate times, like funerals. Perhaps if we were less restrained at other times, we wouldn't have to cut loose at the "wrong" times. But our everyday lives are simply too filled with a multitude of restrictions, from the mundane "Don't walk" to the rather considerable restraints that we all must abide by in order to be deemed "normal," properly socialized people. Play and humor can help us feel momentarily free of these everyday constraints.

Over the course of the next few days, notice the situations in which, as a matter of course, you repress your natural urge to play. Notice when you stop yourself from reaching out to make contact with other people—what makes you pull back? The next time you're in an elevator, notice that you may have an impulse to act differently than usual. Watch yourself resist this impulse, as you force yourself to face front, staring at the illuminated buttons, like everybody else. When you see a baby crawling across the floor, do you feel like getting down on all fours, too, and sharing in the fun? Listen to the voice of civilization telling you to act your age.

Whenever I think about someone who gives himself permission to play at all times, free from the normal social restraints, I invariably think about Jerry Ewen, president of Playfair Canada. The first time I met Jerry he invited me for a twilight stroll through Vancouver, and I soon learned that even walking down the street with Jerry can be an adventure. First he discovered a discarded department-store mannequin in a trash bin, and he started dancing up and down the sidewalk with her. Then he spied an abandoned shopping cart and coaxed me into it, so he could push me and the mannequin madly down the street. Our destination turned out to be his favorite bar, where he parked the cart, and the three of us went inside and ordered up a table.

After a couple of beers, I excused myself to go to the rest room, and when I returned, Jerry and the mannequin were seated at a different table with two attractive single women, and all four of them were waving madly for me to join them. Later that evening, Jerry recounted to me the story of his trip to Montreal the previous winter. He had dined alone in a restaurant where it seemed all the patrons were French-speaking. He was surrounded by diners having animated conversations, but he couldn't understand a word they were saying. One table in particular caught his eye: it seemed to be a birthday party for a man in his late thirties, and all the guests at the party were drinking toasts, laughing, and generally carrying on. What especially intrigued Jerry about this group was that of the fifteen diners around the table, only two of them were men.

This was the kind of party Jerry would have liked to join, but he didn't see how he could talk his way in. So he finished his dinner in silence. As he was ordering dessert, he noticed that the birthday party was ending and that all of the women had lined up to say a final farewell to their host. All of a sudden, Jerry saw a way he could join the party without having to say a word. As the birthday boy was hugging each of his guests good night, Jerry walked over and stood next to him, opened his arms, and pretended that he, too, was part of the reception line. This outrageous gesture immediately earned him a full complement of laughs, giggles, hugs, and kisses from the delighted women. It didn't matter that Jerry couldn't speak a word to them; his open arms were a clear communication that he, too, had come to play.

If you are going to honor your natural impulse to play, you are going to need to give yourself some support to break away from the cultural norms that society expects from a well-socialized adult. So mark a day on your calendar to begin practicing, and when that day comes, whenever the urge to play comes upon you, don't think twice, just go for it.

It's time to go out there and create some memories.

Take
the Pledge

One of my clearest memories from elementary school is the morning ritual of standing with hands over hearts as the class, in unison, gave the Pledge of Allegiance. While loyalty to flag and country are certainly important concepts, for me as a youngster this ritual was rather empty and meaningless. I don't think I fully understood what it was all about. On the other hand, I definitely had a clear idea about play. I didn't need to verbalize my commitment to have fun. Just sound the bell for recess, and I was instantly ready to head out and play.

For adults, things are somehow the other way around. When was the last time someone came by your house, knocked on the door, and invited you out to play? As adults we may understand the need for loyalty to flag and country, but we need to be reminded constantly of the importance of play. Consequently, it is important that we make a pledge to ourselves that we are going to lighten up our lives.

This book has been an attempt to knock on your door—whether the door to your office, your car, or your home—and invite you to a life of laughter and play. If you thumb back through the book, you will find numerous ways to help you answer the invitation. Of course, there are thousands more ways to lighten up your life. However, none will be effective unless you are willing to take the pledge—a pledge that you will live your daily life as play.

I consider myself to be somewhat of an expert when it comes to lightening up; yet, every day I have to retake this pledge to seek out play wherever I can. The first time I had the opportunity to travel to Paris, for example, I had a hard time seeing the trip as an opportunity to play. I was quite worried about how I was going to have a good time in Paris when I could only speak a little French. I had heard lots of stories about how rude and intolerant the French are toward Americans, and that the French really don't like to speak English very much. I really love the English language. I like to talk, and I pride myself on being somewhat articulate. I love hearty conversation and good discussions. I was not looking forward to entering a culture where my vocabulary would be reduced to that of a three-year-old (on my best days). My conversational ability in French was limited to saying brilliant things like "Where is the Louvre?" and "Is this the hotel?" and "Do you serve chicken-fried steak?"

I wanted to make human-to-human contact with the French people, but I was afraid that my feeble use of the language would present an insurmountable barrier. Then I remembered that I had taken the pledge. I just needed to find a way to lighten up about the whole language problem.

I eventually discovered a way to break down the barriers instantly. I would make an appropriate facial expression and begin virtually every conversation with "*Je suis désolé. Je ne parle français pas bien. Je suis chinois.*" ("I am sorry, I don't speak French well. I am Chinese.")

Now, I can be a lot of things, but just by looking at me the French could readily see that one thing I surely couldn't be is Chinese. The reactions of the French people I met were usually the same: a short, stunned silence, followed by a puzzled look that seemed to say, "Does this idiot realize what he just said?" Finally, when they saw the grin on my face, they realized I was playing with them. I had told them a little joke, and so had provided them a window into who I am. They were then more than willing to share themselves with me, to let me come to know them as human beings as well. By recognizing my limitations and making light of them, I was able to spend a wonderful week laughing and playing with the French.

I am very fortunate in the work that I do, since I get so many opportunities to see how laughable my life is. Just a few weeks ago I was giving a presentation at a very swanky retirement home in Dallas. Much of my talk was centered around Plato's injunction that life should be lived as play. After the presentation, one very elderly woman was most effusive in her praise of my lecture. She went on and on about how very meaningful my talk had been to her. I was really beginning to be carried away by her praise when she said, "I especially liked what you said about Pluto."

I smiled to myself at her confusion in thinking of the ancient Greek philosopher as Pluto rather than Plato. Then she said very confidentially, "You know, I went to high school with the man who discovered Pluto." In that instant I realized that she probably had not paid very much attention to this lecture that she thought was so wonderful.

And so it goes. Day after day presenting itself as an opportunity to live lightly and to laugh at ourselves.

Shortly after my book *Managing to Have Fun* was published, I received a fax from Mr. Antti Kerhonen, at the Helsinki University of Technology, in Lahti Centre, Finland. I was quite flattered that someone so far away would be reading my book, and Mr. Kerhonen had obviously studied it quite thoroughly.

In one section of the book I presented fifty-two case studies of ways to have fun at work, one for every week of the year. Mr. Kerhonen was particularly intrigued by one of the examples I offered, that of stopping at a tollbooth and paying the toll not only for your own car but also for the car behind you. After complimenting me profusely on the book, my Finnish fan added that he had "one big complaint to make. We do not have any toll roads here in Finland, so I only got fifty-one good ideas of how to have fun at work. Now, you can either fax me back another idea, or, if you are out of them at the moment, please fax me back forty-two cents, which is the approximate street price of one of your ideas, in Finland!"

No response to my book could have made me happier. Clearly Mr. Kerhonen had understood the true spirit of my work, and he had acted out of that spirit. Not only had he managed to have fun, but he made my day a fun one as well.

There is nothing more that I could wish for you than, like Mr. Kerhonen, you are willing to act on your own playful convictions—that is, that you are willing to take the pledge to let more play into your life every day.

There is no time like the present to lighten up your life. At the start of your next workday, find a room in your house where you can be alone with a mirror. Lock the door, so you won't be disturbed. Get a good look at that playful face staring back at you in the mirror. Put your right hand over your heart, and make a solemn pledge to treat yourself with kindness and forgiveness, all day long. To look for what's not wrong, instead of what's wrong. To take every opportunity to celebrate. To surround yourself with people who like to laugh and play.

And as you get a good look at that playful visage staring back at you in the mirror, let a smile flash across both your faces, as you tell your reflection in no uncertain terms, "I want you to lighten up on me already, will you! Now, let's go to work and have some fun!"

Acknowledgments

Ken Einstein, Amo Tarnoff, and Ritch Davidson all read a version of this work in its infancy, and their scribbled comments in the margins of the manuscript I found helpful time and again.

Over the years when I had stopped working on this project and despaired of ever completing it, Stan Mellin, Andy Mozenter, and my mother, Barbara Weinstein, kept telling me how much they had enjoyed it in its first incarnation, and kept encouraging me to return to it. I am grateful for their unsolicited and repeated encouragement.

Angela Miller once again gave generously of her time and expertise, and helped me conceptualize the final form that pulled this material together.

When I was away on the island, my assistant, Carole Valentino, provided invaluable research assistance from afar, during a time when we could be only voice mail and E-mail phantasms for each other.

My agent, Margret McBride, let me know in no uncertain terms how excited she was about this book, and I played her enthusiastic voice mail message over and over again. Her assistant, Jason Cabassi, did a terrific job of slashing the book proposal down to its essence, mercilessly cutting away pages that I couldn't bear to let go of but that now I can hardly remember.

I had a wonderful connection with my editor, Brian DeFiore, from our very first meeting. Even before I met him, when he was just another name on a long list of possible editors, I had a very strong intuition that he was the one I wanted to work with on this project, and I am delighted that it worked out that way.

Management consultants Mike DiLorenzo and Ken Macher spent many delightful hours during our trek in Nepal exploring the intricacies of "Row, Row, Row Your Boat" with me. I am grateful for their insight, and for all the fun we had hiking together while musing about work and play.

Carol Ann Fried, who is a constant source of innovative training ideas, first introduced me to the practice of "Flowers and Garbage."

I was excited when the time came to show some of these pages to my wife, Geneen. The final draft of this book came together for me on our annual vacation/writing retreat on the island, with Geneen writing upstairs every morning and me writing downstairs, and our cat, Blanche, commuting between the two of us. Geneen's professional reading of the manuscript was most perceptive, as always, and her support for the project was unwavering. I appreciate, too, her bravery and tact in pointing out the parts of the book that didn't work for her.

Finally, the collaboration with my co-author, Luke Barber, was a complete joy from start to finish. I was so delighted by Luke's stories as I would receive each of them that I could often talk of nothing else for days afterward. This was a seamless collaboration; we have rewritten each other's material so many times over the years that by now we can hardly tell who has written what. But that was always our goal: to speak in one voice about some of our shared passions and joys, and to have a project that would bring us the great joy of working and playing together. It did all that.

M.W.

I owe so much to so many people. Thank you.

Lee Paez was a constant source of encouragement and help. She was there for me in every way from the first page of the first draft to the last page of the finished product. She not only championed my efforts, but also held my hand along the way.

Alicia Paez, Kevin Paez, Rachel Barber, Sarah Deering, and Michael Lysobey, while all grown up now, are still my wonderful children. I am so lucky to have them in my life. They taught me some of the greatest lessons I have been blessed to learn.

My friends Steve Mittelstet, John Barrett, and James Hall have helped me for many years in my effort to become a writer. While they are in no way responsible for the skills I still lack, much credit is due to them for what I have been able to achieve.

Steve Graham, Tom O'Brien, and Gary Verett have encouraged me and supported me in ways that they will never know, but in ways that I will never forget.

In my life I have been especially blessed to have teachers, mentors, and models who walked the earth in such a way that my life could not help but be transformed. Leroy Garrett, Florence Wiedeman, and Thich Nhat Hanh are three very special examples.

Sadie, Wicca, Sweet Dreams, Blue, and Casey Bear graciously shared their house with me during the writing of this book and were always there for me when hand or cheek needed to touch fur. Blue was not only a faithful running companion, she was also a daily inspiration.

I am grateful for my friends and colleagues at Richland College. They have provided me with ideas and material for this book, and they have made my work environment a place that is filled each day with laughter and play.

Special thanks to our agent, Margret McBride, our editor, Brian DeFiore, and to all of the talented people at Villard for their excellent work in helping to make this book a reality.

And finally, to my friend and co-author, Matt Weinstein. Without Matt this book could not and would not be. I can not imagine a better person with whom to work and play. Throughout the process, even as we worked like dogs, Matt was always able to flow like water.

L.B.

Index

About the Authors

MATT WEINSTEIN is the founder and Emperor of Playfair Inc., an international management consulting company that presents innovative team-building programs to more than four hundred clients each year. One of the most widely requested speakers on the corporate lecture circuit and a nationally acclaimed expert on the use of play in the workplace, he is the author of *Managing to Have Fun*. He lives in northern California with his wife, Geneen Roth.

LUKE BARBER is a professor of philosophy at Richland College in Dallas, Texas, where he teaches both philosophy and ethics. His innovative teaching earned him recognition by the National Institute of Staff and Organizational Development as a master teacher. His previous careers as a child evangelist, a navy seaman, and a 100-mile ultra-marathon endurance runner have given him a unique perspective on learning to laugh and play with life's problems.

Matt Weinstein and the Playfair senior staff, Ritch Davidson, Fran Solomon, and Terry Sand, are available for speeches and workshops about the uses of fun and play in team building. Topics include:

Work Like Your Dog: How to Work Less, Play More, and Earn More
Putting Fun to Work: The Power of Humor in Business
Managing to Have Fun: How to Reward, Recognize, and Revitalize Your Workforce
Laughter, Stress, and Self-Esteem
Putting the Fun Back in Customer Service
The Improvising Organization

For further information, visit their website at www.Playfair.com or call 1-800-750-5439.

Printed in the United States
70871LV00003B/271